THE GOD ORGASM

Ray Eichenberger

THE GOD ORGASM

Published by Ray Eichenberger

Copyright 2024, Red Foot Racing Stables, LLC

All Rights Assigned to: Red Foot Racing Stables, LLC

RedFootBooks@aol.com

Cover design by Joleene Naylor

Any Bible verses quoted herein are from the King James Version

Ray Eichenberger

DEDICATION

To: Connie- my muse, and Kyle, Stephanie, Hallie, Cole, Leda, Austin and Ellie- praying that you discover the joy of worshipping God

THE GOD ORGASM

Ray Eichenberger

Table of Contents

DEDICATION ii

TO THE READER vi

PROLOGUE 1

DAVID'S JOY IN GOD 4

OLD TESTAMENT JOY 16

SONGS OF JOY 27

JOYFUL GIFTS TO JESUS 40

JOY FROM JESUS 65

JOY AFTER JESUS 91

GOD'S GIFT OF JOY- SEX 119

SEXY SONG OF SOLOMON 138

ETERNAL JOY OF SEX? 157

DAILY JOY IN GOD 173

AN ETERNITY OF JOY 223

ABOUT THE AUTHOR 227

THE GOD ORGASM

Ray Eichenberger

TO THE READER

This book will decidedly not be anything that you can anticipate it will be. The title is provocative, but it will be reverent, based on Scripture, and hopefully will make you consider how you worship our God and think of Him.

I was born and raised into the Lutheran Church. After a brief rebellion from going to church while I was a college student, I returned to the church and have been walking with God since that time. I have, at various times, attended a Grace Brethren Church, and now an unaffiliated, Bible preaching and Bible teaching church for over thirty- five years.

I'm a born again Christian who believes in the inerrancy of the Bible as the inspired Word of God.

You will enjoy this work more if you have a Bible close by to you as I cite Bible verses, some of which will be included in their entirety. All Bible references are from the King James, due to my personal preference and copyright standards while writing. You may enjoy a different Bible version. Please do

THE GOD ORGASM

not permit the use of the King James version to dampen your study of the Scriptures as we go along- you can always settle in with your own favorite translation when we reference Bible verses in this work.

Sit back, open your mind to God and His Spirit, and be prepared to change and challenge the intensity and joy with which you worship God. And, explore with me the joy of our future worship of God when we get to Heaven and begin to commune more intimately with Him

"If thou turn away thy foot from the sabbath, from doing thy pleasure on my holy day; and call the sabbath a delight, the holy of the LORD, honourable; and shalt honour him, not doing thine own ways, nor finding thine own pleasure, nor speaking thine own words: Then shalt thou delight thyself in the LORD; and I will cause thee to ride upon the high places of the earth, and feed thee with the heritage of Jacob thy father: for the mouth of the LORD hath spoken it." Isaiah 58: 13-14.

"Let us be glad and rejoice, and give honour to him: for the marriage of the Lamb is come, and his wife hath made herself ready. And to her was granted that she should be arrayed in fine linen, clean and white: for the fine linen is the righteousness of saints. And he saith unto me, Write, Blessed are they which are called unto the marriage supper of the Lamb. And he saith unto me, These are the true sayings of God." Revelation 19: 7-9

"And I, John saw the holy city, new Jerusalem, coming down from God out of heaven, prepared as a bride and adorned for her husband. And I heard a great voice out of heaven saying, Behold, the tabernacle of God is with men, and he will dwell with them, and they shall be his people, and God himself, shall be with them, and be their God. And God shall wipe away all tears from their eyes; and there shall be no more death, neither sorrow, nor crying, neither shall there be any more pain: for the former things are passed away. And he that sat upon the throne said, Behold, I make all things new. And he said unto me, Write: for these words are true, and faithful. And he said unto me, It is done. I am Alpha and Omega, the beginning and the end. I will give unto him that is athirst of the fountain of the water of life freely. He that overcometh shall inherit all things; and I will be his God and he shall be my son." Revelation 21: 2-7

THE GOD ORGASM

"And the Spirit and the bride say, Come. And let him that heareth say, Come. And let him that is athirst come. And whosoever will, let him take the water of life freely." Revelation 22: 17.

THE GOD ORGASM

PROLOGUE

Checking football scores during worship . . . setting fantasy football lineups during the 9:00 AM service . . . leaving church bored and somewhat upset because of the feeling that the service just didn't speak to me in the way I wanted it to . . . going through the motions and distractedly singing the words to whatever praise and worship song has appeared on the big screens on the sides of the platform at my church, without thinking about what is really going on . . . taking God for granted and not spending time during the week while away from church in Bible study and prayer and worship . . . turning the cell phone alarm off, rolling over in bed, and missing both services at church.

All of the above, and other lazy, apathetic behaviors have sometimes described my Christian walk and worship of God throughout my life. And, even after becoming a more "mature" follower of Christ, I can sometimes find myself reverting to some of the same old, selfish, and bad habits concerning my worship and relationship with God. This book has its impetus and inspiration in the belief that maybe you too have sometimes shared my apathetic and overly "taking for granted" attitude about our joy, obligation, and privilege in worshipping God and the Lord Jesus Christ.

I finally decided that I want the key word to my worship at my now advancing age to be joy- the worship of our God should be full of ecstasy, love, honor, praise and glorifying our Creator. And, I have resolved to make my joyful worship habits seven days a week endeavors, and not just behavior reserved for several hours each Sunday morning. Most of all, we should invoke our joy in worship knowing that we are promised an eternity in Heaven worshipping and communing with God and the Lord Jesus Christ.

THE GOD ORGASM

So, let's go forward as you read this work with an open mind and a sincere quest to drastically alter and reform the manner, method and attitude in which we worship our God.

Ray Eichenberger

DAVID'S JOY IN GOD

Our Bible, particularly in the Old Testament, and sometimes in the New Testament, has excellent examples of the joy and exhilaration that we should encounter as we worship our God. Ironically, the sheer human exaltation in our privilege to worship God sometimes is not overtly apparent in the stories we read in our Bible.

In seeking out examples of joyous worship in the pages of Scripture, one instance immediately came to my memory. It invokes a great story, has a back story as well, and an aftermath of what occurs when we take the worship of God for granted (and criticize others who are more joyful than ourselves).

Caught up in the story of the struggle for power between King Saul and David, and the jealousy of Saul after God instead chose David to be King of Israel, is the fascinating narrative of the history of the Ark of the Covenant during those tumultuous times. When Israel was fighting and contending with the Philistines in the midst of the royal power struggles, King Saul and the people foolishly believed that the presence of the Ark at their battles would alone make them victorious. The mistake of the people concerning the famous Ark was to trust in an object and to ignore the fact that God was displeased with the sins of the nation. The Israelites brought the Ark to their battle camp, but its presence did not bring victory. Instead, "the ark of God was taken, and the two sons of Eli were slain." I Samuel 4: 10.

In I Samuel 5 and 6, God did not tolerate the physical presence of His Ark in the midst of the pagan Philistines, and created signs when the power of the Ark triumphed over the alleged powers of the false Philistine god, Dagon. This led to the situation where the Philistines were terrified of the power and authority of the Holy object, decided that they had to rid themselves of the Ark, and placed it on a cart and sent it down the road and back to Israel, being pulled by two kine and seemingly without a human driver. I Samuel 6.

Long story short, the Ark was recovered without violence or bloodshed, "And the men of Kirjathjearim came, and fetched up the Ark of the Lord, and brought it into the house of Abinadab in the hill, and sanctified Eleazar his son to keep the ark of the Lord." I Samuel 7: 1. The tumult and power struggle between the supporters of Saul, and the supporters of David, resulted in the residence of the Ark in the household of Abinadab for at least twenty years. I Samuel 7: 2.

When David finally solidified his hold on Israel, and came to the point where it was clear that God had given him victory and established his throne, he was determined that he was going to bring the Ark of God out of exile and restore it to a place of reverence in the worship of his God. But, even that decision was not without its dangers and challenges.

"Again, David gathered together all the chosen men of Israel, thirty thousand. And David arose, and went with all the people that were with him from Baale of Judah, to bring up from thence the ark of God, whose name is called by the name of the LORD of hosts that dwelleth between the cherubims. And they set the ark of God upon a new cart, and brought it out of the house of Abinadab that was in Gibeah:

THE GOD ORGASM

and Uzzah and Ahio, the sons of Abinadab, drave the new cart. And they brought it out of the house of Abinadab which was at Gibeah, accompanying the ark of God: and Ahio went before the ark. And David and all the house of Israel played before the LORD on all manner of instruments made of fir wood, even on harps, and on psalteries, and on timbrels, and on cornets, and on cymbals." II Samuel 6: 1-5.

The verses above were the first hint that David's recovery of the Ark was going to be a joyous and exciting event, and it is fairly easy to imagine the festive blasts of the musical instruments when the Ark left the residence of Abinadab.

But, before we get to the main part of our story of worship and exhilaration, a tragic and inexplicable event occurred. "And when they came to Nachon's threshing floor, Uzzah put forth his hand to the ark of God, and took hold of it; for the oxen shook it. And the anger of the LORD was kindled against Uzzah; and God smote him there for his error; and there he died by the ark of God. And David was displeased, because the LORD had made a breach upon Uzzah: and he called the name of the place Perezuzzah to this day. And David was afraid of the LORD that day, and said, How shall the ark of the

LORD come to me? So David would not remove the ark of the LORD unto him into the city of David: but David carried it aside into the house of Obededom the Gittite. And the ark of the LORD continued in the house of Obededom the Gittite three months: and the LORD blessed Obededom, and all his household. And it was told king David, saying, The LORD hath blessed the house of Obededom, and all that pertaineth unto him, because of the ark of God." II Samuel 6: 6-12. "So David went and brought up the ark of God from the house of Obededom into the city of David with gladness." II Samuel 6: 12.

The above passages have little to do with the intensity with which we worship God, and more to do with the holiness of Him and His name. God had decreed when the Ark was first crafted according to His specific instructions that the object was Holy and not to be touched by human hands. Gold plated staves were used from the start of the history of the Ark to carry it as it went along with the Israeli people wandering in the wilderness in the times of Moses and in the aftermath of the flight from Egypt. Exodus 25: 10-16.

THE GOD ORGASM

The joy that David experienced in returning the Ark to Jerusalem, and in thanking and praising God for its safe return to His people, is now very apparent in the following key passages of our theme. "And it was so, that when they that bare the ark of the LORD had gone six paces, he sacrificed oxen and fatlings. And David danced before the LORD with all his might; and David was girded with a linen ephod. So David and all the house of Israel brought up the ark of the LORD with shouting, and with the sound of the trumpet." II Samuel 6: 13-15.

In searching for a cover of this book, I researched artistic impressions of David bringing the Ark back to Jerusalem. Many of these artists viewed the scene in their mind's eye exactly as I have also imagined it to be. I can envision an exhilarated King David, who had shed most of his clothing, dancing half naked in front of the Ark as it made its procession back to Jerusalem. The dance and music were each joyous celebrations and worship of our God, because the Ark was the revered symbol of His power, authority, and providence among and towards the people of Israel.

Ray Eichenberger

Elation is the key word here. David was rejoicing and celebrating his God, and the dance and music were most likely spontaneous outflows of the joy that he felt thanking the Lord and communing with Him. This is the perfect example of the joy of worship that I want to build into my own spiritual life. I'm not suggesting that in every church service we attend on a Sunday morning or at other times throughout the week that we should all strip down nearly half naked, and vigorously dance before God- although that would be a sight to behold. I am emphatically stating that such joy and exhilaration should encompass and embrace our attitudes towards the worship, thanksgiving, and praise that we give to our God and King on a regular basis.

I recently joked with a church friend that I find our services at our church to be too often lacking in such passion, and too often pretty dull and somber as we praise and worship God. I humorously invoked the famous scene from the movie, The Blues Brothers, when I made that statement. You might have seen the scene in the movie- Jake and Elwood, in the midst of their probably very sacrilegious "mission for God," find a church shepherded by James Brown. The all black church

THE GOD ORGASM

was visited by the painfully too white Blues brothers, but we see a great, soulful choir praising God, and excited worshippers responding to the message of the Reverend Brown by doing cartwheels in the aisles in response to the sermon and the great soul music of the choir. As weird as it seems, that is a great visual example of joyous and exhilarated worship. What was probably intended by the writers of the movie to be a satire poking fun at the enthusiasm of evangelical Christians instead struck me as a great example of intense and fun worship.

The other astounding factor in the behavior of King David as he worshipped, praised, and rejoiced in the path of the Holy Ark and in communion with his God was that it was undoubtedly not very royal and appropriate behavior for a great and revered ruler of his people. Kings were supposed to act like kings in the Oriental culture of the times, and were not supposed to make a public spectacle of themselves as they worshipped God or did anything else. That potential factor makes the joyous dancing of David before the Ark even more astounding.

Ray Eichenberger

That very element of expected royal behavior that I just mentioned makes the rest of the story of the entry of the Holy Ark into Jerusalem even more understandable.

"And as the ark of the LORD came into the city of David, Michal Saul's daughter looked through a window, and saw king David leaping and dancing before the LORD; and she despised him in her heart. And they brought in the ark of the LORD, and set it in his place, in the midst of the tabernacle that David had pitched for it: and David offered burnt offerings and peace offerings before the LORD. And as soon as David had made an end of offering burnt offerings and peace offerings, he blessed the people in the name of the LORD of hosts. And he dealt among all the people, even among the whole multitude of Israel, as well to the women as men, to every one a cake of bread, and a good piece of flesh, and a flagon of wine. So all the people departed every one to his house. Then David returned to bless his household. And Michal the daughter of Saul came out to meet David, and said, How glorious was the king of Israel to day, who uncovered himself to day in the eyes of the handmaids of his servants, as one of the vain fellows shamelessly uncovereth himself! And

THE GOD ORGASM

David said unto Michal, It was before the LORD, which chose me before thy father, and before all his house, to appoint me ruler over the people of the LORD, over Israel: therefore will I play before the LORD." II Samuel 6: 16-21.

In the dynamics of husband and wife, and particularly in the tangled love life of King David, there may have been more going on in this relationship than what we know about in the text of II Samuel 6. But, it certainly appears to me as if Michal may have been one of those people who saw the joyous dancing and worship of David and did in fact think that it was unsightly and embarrassing for the King of Israel to carry-on in such a manner, even in an effort to praise and worship God.

David was outraged and angry at the words of his wife, and not only did David rebuke her with the above harsh words spoken to her, but he also had a punishment in store for her and her attitudes that was very long lasting. David said to Michal, "And I will yet be more vile than thus, and will be base in mine own sight: and of the maidservants which thou hast spoken of, of them shall I be had in honour. Therefore Michal the daughter of Saul had no child unto the day of her death." II Samuel 6: 16-23. Michael's words so outraged

David that he presumably stopped having sexual relations with his wife, and she bore no children for the King after that time.

One of the keys in the story of David, his joyful worship before the Ark, and his angry response to the harsh rebuke of Michal, was the word "play." David describes his dancing and worshipping as "play" before the Lord. To fully understand how David used the word "play" in this context, drift back to your own days as a child, when it was joyful and exhilarating merely to run around outside with your friends and to totally exhaust yourself doing things that you loved to do in your young life. This may have been participating in a pick-up game of sports with your buddies, playing a game such as hop-scotch, or simply indulging in what we used to call "chase"- someone was always 'it," and tried to touch (or worse) the other kids who ran around trying to avoid them.

When David used the word "play," he was trying to invoke that youthful joy in physically doing something that we all have loved to do at one time or another in our lives. When David "played" before the Lord, he felt that sensation of joy, and exhilaration at immersing himself in something that he

THE GOD ORGASM

loved- worshipping his God. As we worship the Lord on a Sunday morning, and during our times of worship throughout any given week, we should all seek to emulate David and "play" before God. The next time that you begin to leave the house to go to church on a Sunday morning, tell your family, "Come on, we're going to play before God this morning." They may give you a very quizzical look and expression in return.

In the next chapters of this work, we are going to move forward and seek more examples in Scripture of joyous worship and exhilarating celebration as we come before our God.

Ray Eichenberger

OLD TESTAMENT JOY

I realize that it may be very difficult to convince most of us that our worship of God is way too dispassionate, and way too joyless. Each of us have far different personalities we exhibit throughout our daily routines. Although the content of the passages which came to my mind in this regard are most likely out of context for the topic of fervent worship, they did come to my memory. And, the passages deal with the fact that God does not wish us to be lukewarm and tepid about anything to do with our relationship to Him. "And unto the angel of the church of the Laodiceans write; These things saith the Amen, the faithful and true witness, the beginning of the creation of God; I know thy works, that thou art neither cold nor hot: I would thou wert cold or hot. So then because thou art lukewarm, and neither cold nor hot, I will spue thee out of my mouth. Because thou sayest,

THE GOD ORGASM

I am rich, and increased with goods, and have need of nothing; and knowest not that thou art wretched, and miserable, and poor, and blind, and naked." Revelation 3: 14-17.

God's warning to the Laodiceans may have been about their faith in general, their works, or the overall mission of their new church, but I certainly believe that it also may have been a very relevant warning about their lackluster and apathetic attitudes as they went about regularly worshipping God- they were neither hot or cold about anything.

After II Samuel 6, I then made an extensive search of the Old Testament to find other examples of joyous and exhilarating worship of our God by the nation of Israel and God's people. Joy in worship is certainly present in the Old Testament, but the way that it was expressed may not be capable of being duplicated in our modern worship. Particularly in the stories of the first human beings, and then the patriarchs of the Bible and their successors, joyous worship is often found in the sacrifice of animals and that direct obedience to God as the form and substance of the acts necessary to worship Him. Remember that the Old

Testament describes the actions and aromas of animal sacrifice in that context as a "sweet savour" to God. Genesis 8: 21. As a result, I have often joked that God must have loved a good barbecue.

For example, one of the most joyous events in the Old Testament must have been when Noah was adrift in the Ark after forty days, and finally sent out the dove a penultimate time, which returned with the branch sprig in his mouth. Genesis 8: 8-12. Noah and his family were commanded by God to leave the Ark, and, in their thankfulness and joy, he took from every clean beast and fowl on the Ark (he had brought along extras) and "offered burnt offerings on the altar." Genesis 8: 20.

After the story of Noah, Genesis immediately features God's call of Abraham, and that patriarch's detailed story. When Abraham first passed through the land of Canaan, God appeared to him, and for the first time stated the promise that he would give the land where Abraham was standing to him and his seed. Abraham responded in gratitude to this wonderful news by building an altar to the Lord. Genesis 12: 8.

THE GOD ORGASM

Although there is no mention of Abraham sacrificing animals on this newly erected altar to his God, there are other stories in Genesis about the worship of Abraham. In Genesis 17, God again comes to Abraham and repeats the covenant that the land of Israel will belong to Abraham and his succeeding generations. In a strange twist, and another example of not so commonly joyous worship, God also creates circumcision as a sign of adherence to the gift of the covenant, and Abraham celebrates the blessing and reminder of the covenant by having every male of his household, his son Ishmael, and his servants, circumcised. Genesis 17: 23. Ouch, this seems to me to be a very painful sort of obedience and worship to God, and may not have struck those involved as joyful at the time.

Of course, Abraham became well known for another famous example of joyous worship of God involving an actual sacrifice. In Genesis 22, the famous story of God telling Abraham to sacrifice Isaac as a sign of obedience to Him is told. Genesis 22. God spared the life of Isaac from the sacrifice at literally the last second, as Abraham had the knife in his hand to perform the terrible deed, and had already tied

Isaac to the altar. Genesis 22: 11-12. But, the postscript of the story is that Abraham, in his joy and reverence to God still celebrated God's kindness to him by sacrificing a ram to God, which the Lord had caused to be caught in a nearby thicket by the ram's horns. Genesis 22: 13.

Isaac's son, Jacob, also indulged in this powerful method of praising and worshipping God by using the best celebrations to sacrifice animals. When Jacob left his father-in-law, Laban, with Laban's daughters as his wives, Rachel and Leah, he more or less snuck away, failing to even say his goodbyes. The story in Genesis does not say that Laban minded so much that Jacob had left so hurriedly, but was irate that his daughter, Rachel, had gone away with the family gods (images in Genesis 31). Jacob and Laban could have fought and warred as a result of the circumstances, but God supernaturally protected Jacob from his irate father-in-law by warning Laban in a dream that he should not harm Jacob. Genesis 31: 24.

Laban still overtook Jacob and his family, but after a few tense words, celebrated a covenant between themselves, and solidified the covenant by offering up sacrifices to the God of Jacob. Genesis 31: 54.

A few chapters later in Genesis, God renews the covenant promises given to Abraham and Isaac by repeating the promise of the gift of the land to Jacob. Jacob again celebrates with a sacrifice, this time with a drink offering and the pouring out of oil. Genesis 35: 14.

The exhibition of joyous worship as expressed through animal sacrifice continued in the Old Testament after that time. One of the most exhilarating times for David's son, Solomon, occurred when God permitted Solomon to build the first permanent Temple to Him, so that the use of the old Tabernacle of worship could be discontinued. David had desired to build a permanent Temple to his God before that time, but God refused to permit him to do so, because of David's sin of having a sexual relationship with the married Bathsheba. The joy of dedicating and opening the Temple for Solomon became a massive display of the sacrifice of animals to honor God. I Kings 8: 62-64 says that Solomon sacrificed twenty-two thousand oxen, and one hundred twenty-two thousand sheep on the day of the dedication of the Temple.

I have written extensively about my suppositions concerning the logistics of animal sacrifice in both Jewish Temples, in both the non-fiction and fiction works that I have authored. My conclusion each time has been that Temple Mount in Jerusalem must have been one of the bloodiest, goriest places on earth, with the blood of the animals flowing freely, and with physically gory remnants everywhere resulting from the severing and separating of body parts after the slaying of each animal. Modern man has a very difficult time comprehending the resulting blood and goo, and we would certainly find it next to impossible to find much joy in the worship of God in the midst of such scenes.

There are a few examples in the Old Testament of joyous worship to God without the shedding of blood involved in animal sacrifices. In the book of the prophet Daniel, God gave Daniel, a captive Jew in Babylon, the interpretation of a dream of the King. The King's dream became infamous in the nation, because the King was angry that his supposedly learned advisors and seers could not tell him what the dream meant. When God revealed the meaning of the King's dream to Daniel, the resulting prayer of Daniel was full of joy and worship. Daniel both blessed and worshipped the God of Heaven. "Daniel answered and said, Blessed be the name of God for ever and ever: for wisdom and might are his: And he changeth the times and the seasons: he removeth kings, and setteth up kings: he giveth wisdom unto the wise, and knowledge to them that know understanding: He revealeth the deep and secret things: he knoweth what is in the darkness, and the light dwelleth with him. I thank thee, and praise thee, O thou God of my fathers, who hast given me wisdom and might, and hast made known unto me now what we desired of thee: for thou hast now made known unto us the king's matter." Daniel 2: 20-23.

Another one of the most joyous moments of worship in the Old Testament occurred when Moses, and his sister, Miriam, wanted to celebrate the release of the Israeli slaves from nearly four hundred years of bondage in Egypt, as well as the parting of the Red Sea by God as they fled from the pursuing armies of Pharaoh. The following passages involved music, so notice the references to song and the use of instruments to praise God.

Ray Eichenberger

"Then sang Moses and the children of Israel this song unto the LORD, and spake, saying, I will sing unto the LORD, for he hath triumphed gloriously: the horse and his rider hath he thrown into the sea. The LORD is my strength and song, and he is become my salvation: he is my God, and I will prepare him an habitation; my father's God, and I will exalt him. The LORD is a man of war: the LORD is his name. Pharaoh's chariots and his host hath he cast into the sea: his chosen captains also are drowned in the Red sea. The depths have covered them: they sank into the bottom as a stone. Thy right hand, O LORD, is become glorious in power: thy right hand, O LORD, hath dashed in pieces the enemy. And in the greatness of thine excellency thou hast overthrown them that rose up against thee: thou sentest forth thy wrath, which consumed them as stubble. And with the blast of thy nostrils the waters were gathered together, the floods stood upright as an heap, and the depths were congealed in the heart of the sea. The enemy said, I will pursue, I will overtake, I will divide the spoil; my lust shall be satisfied upon them; I will draw my sword, my hand shall destroy them. Thou didst blow with thy wind, the sea covered them: they sank as lead in the mighty waters. Who is like unto thee, O LORD, among the gods? who is like thee, glorious in holiness, fearful in praises, doing wonders? Thou stretchedst out thy right hand, the earth swallowed them. Thou in thy mercy hast led forth the people which thou hast redeemed: thou hast guided them in thy strength unto thy holy habitation. The people shall hear, and be afraid: sorrow shall take hold on the inhabitants of Palestina. Then the dukes of Edom shall be amazed; the mighty men of Moab, trembling shall take hold upon them; all the inhabitants of Canaan shall melt away. Fear and dread shall fall upon them; by the greatness of thine arm they shall be as still as a stone; till thy people pass over, O LORD, till the people pass over, which thou hast purchased. Thou shalt bring them in, and plant them in the mountain of thine inheritance, in the place, O LORD, which thou hast made for thee to dwell in, in the Sanctuary, O LORD, which thy hands have established. The LORD shall reign for ever and ever. For the horse of Pharaoh went in with his chariots and with his horsemen into the sea, and the LORD brought again the waters of the sea upon them; but the children of Israel went on dry land in the midst of the sea. And Miriam the prophetess, the sister of Aaron, took a timbrel in her hand; and all the women went out after her with timbrels and with dances. And Miriam answered them, Sing ye to the LORD, for he hath triumphed gloriously; the horse and his rider hath he thrown into the sea." Exodus 15: 1-21.

The songs of Moses and Miriam illustrate other forms of exhilarating worship of our God- the use of words and musical instruments to form praises to our Creator. We will discuss the joy of worship with song and instruments as we go along in this work.

THE GOD ORGASM

SONGS OF JOY

I am an avid fan of the Psalms. For whatever mood or circumstance in life you find yourself in at any given moment, there is most likely a Psalm that will speak to you and minister to you. I find despair in the Psalms, anger in the songs, a feeling of abandonment by God, fear of enemies and circumstances, pleas for deliverance from problems and enemies, and regret for disease and death. But, I also find praise and the great joy of worship. Don't forget that the Psalms were originally written and penned to be musical- here again is that use of song and instruments to create awe and wonder as we praise and worship our God.

"Rejoice in the LORD, O ye righteous: for praise is comely for the upright. Praise the LORD with harp: sing unto him with the psaltery and an instrument of ten strings. Sing unto him a new song; play skilfully with a loud noise." Psalm 33:

1-3. This Psalm instructs us to worship in joy, rejoice, and for the first time in the book mentions making music to God on instruments, and with a great deal of noise at that. On Sunday morning at my church service, I used to sit in front of a woman who was from Africa. This wonderful woman, who I have gotten to know somewhat, brings with her to church a tambourine, which she shakes and uses during the service. While at first I was a little startled to hear the instrument in my often staid and laid back normal Sunday morning worship service, I eventually got used to it, and it was fun. This worshiper knows how to make a joyful noise to our God with music.

Psalm 47 states "O clap your hands, all ye people; shout unto God with the voice of triumph. For the LORD most high is terrible; he is a great King over all the earth. He shall subdue the people under us, and the nations under our feet. He shall choose our inheritance for us, the excellency of Jacob whom he loved. Selah. God is gone up with a shout, the LORD with the sound of a trumpet. Sing praises to God, sing praises: sing praises unto our King, sing praises. For God is the King of all the earth: sing ye praises with understanding. God reigneth over the heathen: God sitteth upon the throne of his holiness. The princes of the people are gathered together, even the people of the God of Abraham: for the shields of the earth belong unto God: he is greatly exalted." Psalm 47.

Psalm 47 gives many images to us of the joy of worship. We are told to worship God by clapping our hands- in our modern day, applause is considered to be the most common and maybe best form of praise to someone. Conversely, we are told to shout to our God as well. Clapping and shouting during the church service that I attend would be a very uncommon event, but might be necessary some Sunday mornings to wake up the attendees at the early service. Finally, the Psalm tells us to once again add the sounds of instruments to our worship of God. As a former musician on the trumpet back in the day, I have always thought that the resonant tones of that instrument are beautiful to hear. In fact, the Lutheran church where I grew up almost always had trumpets and other brass instruments as a part of the Christmas and Easter holiday celebrations.

Psalm 64 then illustrates a little different form of worship. "I will lift up my hands in thy name. My soul shall be satisfied as with marrow and fatness; and my mouth shall praise thee with joyful lips: When I remember thee upon my bed, and meditate on thee in the night watches. Because thou hast been my help, therefore in the shadow of thy wings will I rejoice. My soul followeth hard after thee: thy right hand upholdeth me. But those that seek my soul, to destroy it, shall go into the lower parts of the earth. They shall fall by the sword: they shall be a portion for foxes. But the king shall rejoice in God; every one that sweareth by him shall glory: but the mouth of them that speak lies shall be stopped." Psalm 64: 4-11. The lifting of our hands to God in worship is specifically called for in this song of David. Raising hands in worship to God is a foreign display of worship in many denominations, and it was something that I wasn't used to when I started to go to a more fundamental church many years ago. Once again, raising our hands to God is something else that can be done to signify the exhilaration and submission to God in worship. We'll discuss that more in depth later. Psalm 64 also contains very vivid imagery that even the King of Israel was supposed to be joyous in the worship of God. Psalm 64: 11.

THE GOD ORGASM

Psalm 89 then instructs us to sing to the Lord. "I will sing of the mercies of the LORD for ever: with my mouth will I make known thy faithfulness to all generations." Psalm 89: 1. "In thy name shall they rejoice all the day: and in thy righteousness shall they be exalted." Psalm 89: 16.

Singing is a very easy action for all of us to perform with great joy and gusto. For those of us who claim that we cannot sing, God doesn't judge the quality of the sound, but He judges the joy of worship and the heart in doing so. Even what you claim to be your mediocre voice is a sweet and desirable sound to our God. We will also discuss more about singing later in this work.

Psalm 92 gives us specific instructions on how to worship our God. "It is a good thing to give thanks unto the LORD, and to sing praises unto thy name, O Most High: To shew forth thy lovingkindness in the morning, and thy faithfulness every night, Upon an instrument of ten strings, and upon the psaltery; upon the harp with a solemn sound. For thou, LORD, hast made me glad through thy work: I will triumph in the works of thy hands." Psalm 92: 1-4. In this Psalm, the instruments are more on the mellow and pretty side of the musical spectrum- stringed instruments, including the harp.

Psalm 95 again commands that we make a joyful noise to the God in our worship. "O come, let us sing unto the LORD: let us make a joyful noise to the rock of our salvation. Let us come before his presence with thanksgiving, and make a joyful noise unto him with psalms. For the LORD is a great God, and a great King above all gods." Psalm 95: 1-3. Note that this song uses our word, "joyful," several times.

Psalm 96 is a complete statement of the way and manner in which we are commanded to worship God. "O sing unto the LORD a new song: sing unto the LORD, all the earth. Sing unto the LORD, bless his name; shew forth his salvation from day to day. Declare his glory among the heathen, his wonders among all people. For the LORD is great, and greatly to be praised: he is to be feared above all gods. For all the gods of the nations are idols: but the LORD made the heavens. Honour and majesty are before him: strength and beauty are in his sanctuary. Give unto the LORD, O ye kindreds of the people, give unto the LORD glory and strength. Give unto the LORD the glory due unto his name: bring an offering, and

THE GOD ORGASM

come into his courts. O worship the LORD in the beauty of holiness: fear before him, all the earth. Say among the heathen that the LORD reigneth: the world also shall be established that it shall not be moved: he shall judge the people righteously. Let the heavens rejoice, and let the earth be glad; let the sea roar, and the fulness thereof. Let the field be joyful, and all that is therein: then shall all the trees of the wood rejoice. Before the LORD: for he cometh, for he cometh to judge the earth: he shall judge the world with righteousness, and the people with his truth." Psalm 96. Notice that the verbs in this song denote activity and action- sing, declare, worship, praise. The song is instructing us that sitting on a pew or chair half asleep on a Sunday morning is directly contrary to the method in which God wants to be worshipped. Our joyful worship is to involve action and is meant to be active.

Psalm 98 states, "O sing unto the Lord a new song; for he hath done marvellous things: his right hand, and his holy arm, hath gotten him the victory. The LORD hath made known his salvation: his righteousness hath he openly shewed in the sight of the heathen. He hath remembered his mercy and his truth toward the house of Israel: all the ends of the earth have seen the salvation of our God. Make a joyful noise unto the LORD, all the earth: make a loud noise, and rejoice, and sing praise. Sing unto the LORD with the harp; with the harp, and the voice of a psalm. With trumpets and sound of cornet make a joyful noise before the LORD, the King. Let the sea roar, and the fulness thereof; the world, and they that dwell therein. Let the floods clap their hands: let the hills be joyful together. Before the LORD; for he cometh to judge the earth: with righteousness shall he judge the world, and the people with equity." Psalm 98. Once again I am struck by the action and activity called for in this Psalm. In worshipping our God, we are told to sing, clap, and be joyful. Anything to do with musical instruments moves me in that manner.

"O God, my heart is fixed; I will sing and give praise, even with my glory. Awake, psaltery and harp: I myself will awake early. I will praise thee, O LORD, among the people: and I will sing praises unto thee among the nations. For thy mercy is great above the heavens: and thy truth reacheth unto the clouds. Be thou exalted, O God, above the heavens: and thy glory above all the earth; That thy beloved may be delivered: save with thy right hand, and answer me. God hath spoken in his holiness; I will rejoice, I will divide Shechem, and mete out the valley of Succoth. Gilead is mine; Manasseh is mine; Ephraim also is the strength of mine head; Judah is my lawgiver; Moab is my washpot; over Edom will I cast out my shoe; over Philistia will I triumph. Who will bring me into the strong city? who will lead me into Edom? Wilt not thou, O God, who hast cast us off? and wilt not thou, O God, go forth with our hosts? Give us help from trouble: for vain is the help of man. Through God we shall do valiantly: for he it is that shall tread down our enemies." Psalm 108. This Psalm again calls for the use of musical instruments, and instructs us to spread our joy in worship beyond our churches on Sunday morning to the "nations."

"O give thanks unto the LORD; for he is good: because his mercy endureth for ever. (1) This is the day which the LORD hath made; we will rejoice and be glad in it. (24) Save now, I beseech thee, O LORD: O LORD, I beseech thee, send now prosperity. (25) Blessed be he that cometh in the name of the LORD: we have blessed you out of the house of the LORD." Psalm 118: 1 and 24-25. Psalm 118 was supposedly a favorite of the disciples of Jesus as they trekked around Israel to minister with their Lord. The best portion of the Psalm to me is that it exhorts us to be joyful and be glad every day- the worship of our God is a continuous, twenty-four hours a day frame of mind.

"Praise ye the LORD. Praise the LORD, O my soul. While I live will I praise the LORD: I will sing praises unto my God while I have any being. Put not your trust in princes, nor in the son of man, in whom there is no help. His breath goeth forth, he returneth to his earth; in that very day his thoughts perish. Happy is he that hath the God of Jacob for his help, whose hope is in the LORD his God: Which made heaven, and earth, the sea, and all that therein is: which keepeth truth for ever: Which executeth judgment for the oppressed: which giveth food to the hungry. The LORD looseth the prisoners: The LORD openeth the eyes of the blind: the LORD raiseth them that are bowed down: the LORD loveth the righteous: The LORD preserveth the strangers; he relieveth the fatherless and widow: but the way of the wicked he turneth upside down. The LORD shall reign for ever, even thy God, O Zion, unto all generations. Praise ye the LORD." Psalm 146. Psalm 146 may have the absolute best line of the praise and joy

THE GOD ORGASM

Psalms- "While I live will I praise the LORD: I will sing praises unto my God while I have any being." Psalm 146: 2.

"Praise ye the LORD. Praise ye the LORD from the heavens: praise him in the heights. Praise ye him, all his angels: praise ye him, all his hosts. Praise ye him, sun and moon: praise him, all ye stars of light. Praise him, ye heavens of heavens, and ye waters that be above the heavens. Let them praise the name of the LORD: for he commanded, and they were created. He hath also stablished them for ever and ever: he hath made a decree which shall not pass. Praise the LORD from the earth, ye dragons, and all deeps: Fire, and hail; snow, and vapours; stormy wind fulfilling his word: Mountains, and all hills; fruitful trees, and all cedars: Beasts, and all cattle; creeping things, and flying fowl: Kings of the earth, and all people; princes, and all judges of the earth: Both young men, and maidens; old men, and children: Let them praise the name of the LORD: for his name alone is excellent; his glory is above the earth and heaven. He also exalteth the horn of his people, the praise of all his saints; even of the children of Israel, a people near unto him. Praise ye the LORD." Psalm 148. This Psalm paints a vivid picture of all of creation and all of nature reveling in joy, worship, and praise to our God. Notice that the elements of praise and worship include the moon, the stars, the planets, all natural creations such as mountains and hills, and then even the animals of our world.

"Praise ye the LORD. Sing unto the LORD a new song, and his praise in the congregation of saints. Let Israel rejoice in him that made him: let the children of Zion be joyful in their King. Let them praise his name in the dance: let them sing praises unto him with the timbrel and harp. For the LORD taketh pleasure in his people: he will beautify the meek with salvation. Let the saints be joyful in glory: let them sing aloud upon their beds. Let the high praises of God be in their mouth, and a two-edged sword in their hand; To execute vengeance upon the heathen, and punishments upon the people; To bind their kings with chains, and their nobles with fetters of iron; To execute upon them the judgment written: this honour have all his saints. Praise ye the LORD." Psalm 149

"Praise ye the LORD. Praise God in his sanctuary: praise him in the firmament of his power. Praise him for his mighty acts: praise him according to his excellent greatness. Praise

THE GOD ORGASM

him with the sound of the trumpet: praise him with the psaltery and harp. Praise him with the timbrel and dance: praise him with stringed instruments and organs. Praise him upon the loud cymbals: praise him upon the high sounding cymbals. Let every thing that hath breath praise the LORD. Praise ye the LORD." Psalm 150. The final two Psalms of the Old Testament continue to paint a vivid portrait of worship and what our attitudes towards our God should be. The words praise, rejoice, and the use of instruments once again should teach us that the sky should be the limit in how and when we worship God. Most importantly, I find the great instruction of the Psalms for us to be that joyful interaction with God, and the duty to lift our praises to God, are not just a Sunday morning ritual, but should be daily habits of constant acknowledgment and worship of our Creator.

Ray Eichenberger

JOYFUL GIFTS TO JESUS

As we leave the study of worship and joy in the Old Testament, and turn to the New Testament, we will discover many more examples of the joyful and exuberant worship of God. And, we should expect the New Testament to be full of such instances- the arrival of Jesus, the Son of God, to our world, and the fulfillment of prophecy and God's plan for us, would certainly have been a glorious and wondrous time for the people who were privileged to experience it.

The mind sets and experiences of the people most intimately involved in the arrival of Jesus to earth in the Christmas story are vivid, and sometimes even under-stated. The Bible really doesn't describe the joy and awe of Mary and Joseph very well sometimes, as they were each visited by angels and told of the pending arrival of the Son of God into their lives. Sometimes we must use our imaginations to revel in the mindsets of Mary and Joseph as they processed the news of the pending arrival of the Son of God, and then lived through all of the events. It's not too difficult to understand the minds of Joseph and Mary under such circumstances. I can imagine the emotions of awe, disbelief, confusion, and uncertainty would have filled both Mary and Joseph at such unexpected news. If it were me, I would certainly be thinking on the part of each of them that it was going to be a daunting and challenging task to serve as the earthly parents to the Son of God. Fear of not quite being ready or up to the task at hand would certainly strike me under such circumstances. Unworthiness would be a constant fear.

But, we do have a vivid insight into the mind set of Mary after the news and under the expectation of what would soon occur when she traveled to visit her cousin, Elisabeth, during her pregnancy. "And Mary said, My soul doth magnify the Lord, And my spirit hath rejoiced in God my Saviour. For he hath regarded the low estate of his handmaiden: for, behold, from henceforth all generations shall call me blessed. For he that is mighty hath done to me great things; and holy is his name. And his mercy is on them that fear him from generation to generation. He hath shewed strength with his arm; he hath scattered the proud in the imagination of their hearts. He hath put down the mighty from their seats, and exalted them of low degree. He hath filled the hungry with good things; and the rich he hath sent empty away. He hath helped his servant Israel, in remembrance of his mercy; As he spake to our fathers, to Abraham, and to his seed for ever. Luke 1: 46-53.

This joyous song of Mary occurred immediately as she entered the house of Elisabeth during her trip. Another one of my favorite passages of the Christmas story had directly preceded this occurrence. When Elisabeth first saw the pregnant Mary, Luke states that, "when Elisabeth heard the salutation of Mary, the babe leaped in her womb; and Elisabeth was filled with the Holy Ghost." Luke 1: 41. Of course, the baby being carried by Elisabeth was only six months or so older than the pregnancy of Mary, and was none other than John the Baptist of the New Testament. The narrative of John the Baptist reacting in the womb to hearing Mary's voice, and then realizing that he was in the presence of the Son of God, is awesome and inspiring. What's more joyful than leaping, and the verse also says that Elisabeth was filled with the Holy Ghost.

I am someone who has always loved the Christmas season for many reasons- the traditions, the bright lights, the stories surrounding the arrival of Jesus to us. The joy of the non-family members who encountered the arrival of baby Jesus does seem to jump off the pages of our Bible. In Luke 2, the first group of this category of people who met and welcomed baby Jesus into the world were the shepherds tending their flocks outside of Bethlehem. Their story is so familiar that I shouldn't repeat it here, but I will just because it involves some of my favorite verses from the Bible. "And there were in the same country shepherds abiding in the field, keeping watch over their flock by night. And, lo, the angel of the Lord came upon them, and the glory of the Lord shone round about them: and they were sore afraid. And the angel said unto them, Fear not: for, behold, I bring you good tidings of great joy, which shall be to all people. For unto you is born this day in the city of David a Saviour, which is Christ the Lord. And this shall be a sign unto you; Ye shall find the babe wrapped in swaddling clothes, lying in a manger. And suddenly there was with the angel a multitude of the heavenly host praising God, and saying, Glory to God in the highest, and on earth peace, good will toward men. And it came to pass, as the angels were gone away from them into heaven, the shepherds said one to another, Let us now go even unto Bethlehem, and see this thing which is come to pass, which the Lord hath made known unto us. And they came with haste, and found Mary, and Joseph, and the babe lying in a manger. Luke 2: 8-16.

The shepherds had every reason to be joyful. And, I've always believed that their joy must have been just a little tempered at the fear and wonder which accompanied the appearance of one angel (they were "sore" afraid, according to Luke, and Linus, of Peanuts fame), then many angels, and being sung to by these Heavenly beings- it must have been fantastic. Then, they had the privilege to walk into Bethlehem (they most likely ran), and they had the unique, first opportunity to view, witness, and meet their God.

The crescendo and end of their story is just as amazing as the visit from the angels. The shepherds were so full of joy and glorious worship at what they had seen and experienced that they became the first evangelists, spreading the good news of the arrival of our Lord and Savior to other people. "And when they had seen it, they made known abroad the saying which was told them concerning this child. And all they that heard it wondered at those things which were told them by the shepherds. But Mary kept all these things, and pondered them in her heart. And the shepherds returned, glorifying and praising God for all the things that they had heard and seen, as it was told unto them." Luke 2: 17-20.

The next group of people who joyfully encountered the infant Jesus were separate individuals with very similar stories. First, an elderly man had been led by God to spend time in the Temple in Jerusalem, anxiously awaiting the arrival of the longed-for Messiah. Mary and Joseph had to take baby Jesus to the Temple to satisfy the rites and requirements towards a Jewish new born male in the Mosaic law. Luke again paints a very vivid picture of this scene. "And when eight days were accomplished for the circumcising of the child, his name was called JESUS, which was so named of the angel before he was conceived in the womb. And when the days of her purification according to the law of Moses were accomplished, they brought him to Jerusalem, to present him to the Lord; (As it is written in the law of the LORD, Every male that openeth the womb shall be called holy to the Lord;) And to offer a sacrifice according to that which is said in the law of the Lord, A pair of turtledoves, or two young pigeons. And, behold, there was a man in Jerusalem, whose name was Simeon; and the same man was just and devout, waiting for the consolation of Israel: and the Holy Ghost was upon him. And it was revealed unto him by the Holy Ghost, that he should not see death, before he had seen the Lord's Christ. And he came by the Spirit into the temple: and when the parents brought in the child Jesus, to do for him after the custom of the law, Then took he him up in his arms, and blessed God, and said, Lord, now lettest thou thy servant depart in peace, according to thy word: For mine eyes have seen thy salvation, Which thou hast prepared before the face of all people; A light to lighten the Gentiles, and the glory of thy people Israel. And Joseph and his mother marvelled at those things which were spoken of him. And Simeon blessed them, and said unto Mary his mother, Behold, this child is set for the fall and rising again of many in Israel; and for a sign which shall be spoken against; (Yea, a sword shall pierce through thy own soul also), that the thoughts of many hearts may be revealed." Luke 2: 21-35.

The words of Simeon in this story have always been very familiar to me, as the Lutheran church of my youth used part of it as the benediction to close most services- "now lettest thou thy servant to depart in peace, according to thy word." Luke 2: 29.

Remarkably, after the Holy Couple and Jesus encountered Simeon, there was another person, this time an elderly woman, who was also frequenting the Temple after being told that she too would encounter the promised Messiah. We are not told by Luke how long these two individuals hung out in the Temple just waiting in excitement and great expectation for the visit from their infant God, but I've always believed that the story gets better as I imagine that they were eagerly waiting for days or weeks on end. "And there was one Anna, a prophetess, the daughter of Phanuel, of the tribe of Aser: she was of a great age, and had lived with an husband seven years from her virginity; And she was a widow of about fourscore and four years, which departed not from the temple, but served God with fastings and prayers night and day. And she coming in that instant gave thanks likewise unto the Lord, and spake of him to all them that looked for redemption in Jerusalem." Luke 2: 36-38.

I've always wondered how both Simeon and Anna recognized baby Jesus as the promised Messiah when the Holy family walked into the Temple. Certainly, the Holy Spirit probably spoke to each of them personally, but how, and in what manner and form?. At times when reading their stories in Luke, my mind can imagine the infant Jesus entering the Temple, and the halo and aura of light often depicted in Renaissance art as being around the head of Jesus, and or atop His forehead, suddenly appears to the worshippers in the building. That will be another video to watch when we all get to Heaven.

The final example of the joy of the people who were led to encounter baby Jesus is found in the three Magi who traveled a long, long way to worship Jesus after He was born. The Bible does not tell us exactly when these three men arrived in Bethlehem to end and complete their journey, but they most likely did not arrive on the night of the Savior's birth, and did not comply with my mother's traditional Nativity scene on the mantle of our house during the Christmas season by joining the shepherds at the manger that first Christmas early morning. I was quite sad when I first learned that historical fact about the night of the birth of Jesus. Matthew 2: 11 tells us that the Magi found Jesus, Mary, and Joseph in a house, not in their cave stable. The story of the Magi is just as familiar to us as the story of the shepherds, but the fascinating part of their role is that, whenever the Magi finally arrived, the star in the sky had led them, and was visible for a long time after the birth of Jesus.

The travelers had every reason to be joyful and excited when they finally discovered and found baby Jesus, since they had expended a great deal of time and effort to come and worship Him. Matthew describes their experience in a few, short verses. "When they had heard the king, they departed; and, lo, the star, which they saw in the east, went before them, till it came and stood over where the young child was. When they saw the star, they rejoiced with exceeding great joy. And when they were come into the house, they saw the young child with Mary his mother, and fell down, and worshipped him: and when they had opened their treasures, they presented unto him gifts; gold, and frankincense and myrrh." Matthew 2: 9-11. As with some of the Psalms concerning worship, we should notice the verbs that are active in the language to describe the behavior of the Wise Men- they rejoiced, they worshipped. There is no reason why our own worship and time spent with our God should not be just as passionate and joyful.

After Jesus began His ministry, there are more examples of joy among the people who were privileged to be a part of the visit of the Son of God to Earth. The first instance of this was when Jesus went to his cousin, John the Baptist, to be baptized in the Jordan River. When Jesus came to John, the Baptist's first reaction was that he had no business baptizing or doing any earthly ritual on behalf of the Son of God.

"Then cometh Jesus from Galilee to Jordan unto John, to be baptized of him. But John forbad him, saying, I have need to be baptized of thee, and comest thou to me? And Jesus answering said unto him, Suffer it to be so now: for thus it becometh us to fulfil all righteousness. Then he suffered him. And Jesus, when he was baptized, went up straightway out of the water: and, lo, the heavens were opened unto him, and he saw the Spirit of God descending like a dove, and lighting upon him: And lo a voice from heaven, saying, This is my beloved Son, in whom I am well pleased." Matthew 3: 13-17. The humility of both John the Baptist and Jesus strikes me in this passage, as well as the fact that Heaven and the Father Himself rejoiced at the undoubtedly unnecessary obedience of the Son in participating in this earthly spiritual ritual.

Although the Scriptural passages in the Gospels don't convey it all that well, I can also imagine this scene and envision the joy of John the Baptist when Jesus came to him to be baptized. The act must have been a sign to the Baptist that Jesus at last was going to begin His ministry in earnest, and would begin to fulfill the mission that the two cousins from their infancy had been instructed about by their God. Perhaps there was also more than a little bit of melancholy in the mind of John, because he was undoubtedly aware of what his own fate would be now that Jesus was there to undertake His ministry.

Other vivid examples of the joy that Jesus brought to people during His ministry are found in the reactions of those individuals who had their lives completely changed by the

Lord when He healed their various illnesses and maladies. "And when Jesus departed thence, two blind men followed him, crying, and saying, Thou son of David, have mercy on us. And when he was come into the house, the blind men came to him: and Jesus saith unto them, Believe ye that I am able to do this? They said unto him, Yea, Lord. Then touched he their eyes, saying, According to your faith be it unto you. And their eyes were opened; and Jesus straitly charged them, saying, See that no man know it. But they, when they were departed, spread abroad his fame in all that country." Matthew 9: 27-31. These verses are typical for the healings and some other miracles of Jesus. The Lord's admonition to the individuals who had just been cured to tell no man of the performing of the miracle wasn't ever too likely to happen. Friends, family, and acquaintances of the formerly blind men were certain to notice that the individuals who were always sightless before were now suddenly restored to their vision. And, these men took it a step further, ignored the instructions of Jesus, and joyfully told everyone in the region what had happened to them and who had performed the miracle.

THE GOD ORGASM

The healed men already exhibited extreme faith in coming to Jesus- their behaviors in calling out to Him as the "son of David" were an acknowledgment that they believed Him to be the Messiah.

Blindness in the population during the time of Jesus was a common theme. Whatever the status of primitive medicine was in turn of the millennium Israel at the time of the Lord, the functioning and care of the eyes might well have been the most misunderstood and the least manageable. Decaying eyesight and blindness must always have been a permanent condition. In his Gospel, Luke, the physician, mentions more about the medical miracles of Jesus than his counterparts- it was a natural area of his interest. Luke also mentions a miracle of Jesus when he again restored the eyesight of an individual. "And it came to pass, that as he was come nigh unto Jericho, a certain blind man sat by the way side begging: And hearing the multitude pass by, he asked what it meant. And they told him, that Jesus of Nazareth passeth by. And he cried, saying, Jesus, thou son of David, have mercy on me. And they which went before rebuked him, that he should hold his peace: but he cried so much the more, Thou son of David, have mercy on me. And Jesus stood, and commanded him to be brought unto him: and when he was come near, he asked him, Saying, What wilt thou that I shall do unto thee? And he said, Lord, that I may receive my sight. And Jesus said unto him, Receive thy sight: thy faith hath saved thee. And immediately he received his sight, and followed him, glorifying God: and all the people, when they saw it, gave praise unto God." Luke 18: 35-43. Notice that this man when cured of his malady was not told by Jesus to be silent, and to keep the act under wraps. In any event, he would not leave the side of the Lord after being cured, and expressed his joy by constantly praising God. The joy of this man was predictable in the story- he again called Jesus by the Messianic name Son of David, even before Jesus paused to help him.

Leprosy was seemingly the other chronic health condition in the time of Jesus which physically debilitated people. It was not only a dread disease physically for the victim, but it was considered contagious enough that lepers were unclean and ostracized from the rest of society. And, this seemingly harsh treatment towards lepers was sanctioned in the laws of God as given to Moses, to protect the health and well-being of others. Leviticus 13. As a result, more of the miracles of Jesus confront that disease as well. Once again, Lute narrates the following story about Jesus and leprosy. "And it came to pass, as he went to Jerusalem, that he passed through the midst of Samaria and Galilee. And as he entered into a certain village, there met him ten men that were lepers, which stood afar off: And they lifted up their voices, and said, Jesus, Master, have mercy on us. And when he saw them, he said unto them, Go shew yourselves unto the priests. And it came to pass, that, as they went, they were cleansed. And one of them, when he saw that he was healed, turned back, and with a loud voice glorified God, And fell down on his face at his feet, giving him thanks: and he was a Samaritan. And Jesus answering said, Were there not ten cleansed? but where are the nine? There are not found that returned to give glory to God, save this stranger. And he said unto him, Arise, go thy way: thy faith hath made thee whole." Luke 17: 11-19. Once again, it is seemingly a very easy thing to be joyful after God cures you of a lifelong, debilitating, and chronic health problem. But, Luke's story of the ten victims of leprosy is very curious in that he narrates that only one of them expressed his joy to

Jesus. And, the most joyous and worshipful beneficiary of the healing power of Jesus was a Samaritan, the offshoot group of Jews usually hated by mainline Jews. This outcast Samaritan fell at the feet of Jesus in joy, and worshipped him after he was the beneficiary of the miracle. This is one of many examples of Jesus demonstrating the exemplary behavior of the often ostracized and hated Samaritan people.

Curiously, the New Testament gospels also record the greatest miracles of all, the various resurrections of the dead by Jesus, but largely fail to record them as joyous events. This would include the raising of Jairus' daughter in Luke 8, and the raising of the ruler's son from afar in John 4. But, it would be difficult to believe that returning someone to life from death was not a joyful occurrence for the family and friends involved. The families of the person restored to life, and the formerly dead individuals themselves, must have been very exuberant, and shocked as well. The joy found in the return to life of a loved one most likely was first preceded by fear and awe that the miracle occurred in the first place.

The joy created when Jesus raised the dead is exhibited and demonstrated in several passages of Scripture. Perhaps my

THE GOD ORGASM

favorite involved the chance meeting of Jesus (or was it?) when he came upon a funeral procession outside of Nain. Just because Jesus happened to be passing by at the time, lives were changed.

"And it came to pass the day after, that he went into a city called Nain; and many of his disciples went with him, and much people. Now when he came nigh to the gate of the city, behold, there was a dead man carried out, the only son of his mother, and she was a widow: and much people of the city was with her. And when the Lord saw her, he had compassion on her, and said unto her, Weep not. And he came and touched the bier: and they that bare him stood still. And he said, Young man, I say unto thee, Arise. And he that was dead sat up, and began to speak. And he delivered him to his mother. And there came a fear on all: and they glorified God, saying, That a great prophet is risen up among us; and, That God hath visited his people. And this rumour of him went forth throughout all Judaea, and throughout all the region round about." Luke 7: 11-17.

The passage says nothing about joy, per se, but does mention that the witnesses to this great event were afraid (no doubt), and that they "glorified" God. I find giving glory to God very joyful, and the return of someone from the dead must have been a time of great exhilaration. Personally, I'd be asking the formerly deceased person where they had been all that time and what they experienced and witnessed.

By far, my favorite Bible story of Jesus resurrecting someone, and the reactions which followed is the raising of Lazarus. John gives the only detailed explanation of this event. I love the story so much that I'll repeat it in its entirety here.

"Now a certain man was sick, named Lazarus, of Bethany, the town of Mary and her sister Martha. (It was that Mary which anointed the Lord with ointment, and wiped his feet with her hair, whose brother Lazarus was sick.) Therefore his sisters sent unto him, saying, Lord, behold, he whom thou lovest is sick. When Jesus heard that, he said, This sickness is not unto death, but for the glory of God, that the Son of God might be glorified thereby. Now Jesus loved Martha, and her sister, and Lazarus. When he had heard therefore that he was sick, he abode two days still in the same place where he was. Then after that saith he to his disciples, Let us go into Judaea again. His disciples say unto him, Master, the Jews of late sought to stone thee; and goest thou thither again? Jesus answered, Are there not twelve hours in the day? If any man walk in the day, he stumbleth not, because he seeth the light of this world. But if a man walk in the night, he stumbleth, because there is no light in him. These things said he: and after that he saith unto them, Our friend Lazarus sleepeth; but I go, that I may awake him out of sleep. Then said his disciples, Lord, if he sleep, he shall do well. Howbeit Jesus spake of his death: but they thought that he had spoken of taking of rest in sleep. Then said Jesus unto them plainly, Lazarus is dead. And I am glad for your sakes that I was not there, to the intent ye may believe; nevertheless let us go unto him. Then said Thomas, which is called Didymus, unto his fellow disciples, Let us also go, that we may die with him. Then when Jesus came, he found that he had lain in the grave four days already. Now Bethany was nigh unto Jerusalem, about fifteen furlongs off: And many of the Jews came to Martha and Mary, to comfort them concerning their brother. Then Martha, as soon as she heard that Jesus was coming, went and met him: but Mary sat still in the house. Then said Martha unto Jesus,

Ray Eichenberger

Lord, if thou hadst been here, my brother had not died. But I know, that even now, whatsoever thou wilt ask of God, God will give it thee. Jesus saith unto her, Thy brother shall rise again. Martha saith unto him, I know that he shall rise again in the resurrection at the last day. Jesus said unto her, I am the resurrection, and the life: he that believeth in me, though he were dead, yet shall he live: And whosoever liveth and believeth in me shall never die. Believest thou this? She saith unto him, Yea, Lord: I believe that thou art the Christ, the Son of God, which should come into the world. And when she had so said, she went her way, and called Mary her sister secretly, saying, The Master is come, and calleth for thee. As soon as she heard that, she arose quickly, and came unto him. Now Jesus was not yet come into the town, but was in that place where Martha met him. The Jews then which were with her in the house, and comforted her, when they saw Mary, that she rose up hastily and went out, followed her, saying, She goeth unto the grave to weep there. Then when Mary was come where Jesus was, and saw him, she fell down at his feet, saying unto him, Lord, if thou hadst been here, my brother had not died. When Jesus therefore saw her weeping, and the Jews also weeping which came with her, he groaned in the spirit, and was troubled. And said, Where have ye laid him? They said unto him, Lord, come and see. Jesus wept. Then said the Jews, Behold how he loved him! And some of them said, Could not this man, which opened the eyes of the blind, have caused that even this man should not have died? Jesus therefore again groaning in himself cometh to the grave. It was a cave, and a stone lay upon it. Jesus said, Take ye away the stone. Martha, the sister of him that was dead, saith unto him, Lord, by this time he stinketh: for he hath been dead four days. Jesus saith unto her, Said I not unto thee, that, if thou wouldest believe, thou shouldest see the glory of God? Then they took away the stone from the place where the dead was laid. And Jesus lifted up his eyes, and said, Father, I thank thee that thou hast heard me. And I knew that thou hearest me always: but because of the people which stand by I said it, that they may believe that thou hast sent me. And when he thus had spoken, he cried with a loud voice, Lazarus, come forth. And he that was dead came forth, bound hand and foot with graveclothes: and his face was bound about with a napkin. Jesus saith unto them, Loose him, and let him go. Then many of the Jews which came to Mary, and had seen the things which Jesus did, believed on him." John 11: 1-45.

The Resurrection of Lazarus resulted in many different reactions. John is quick to narrate that many believed that Jesus was the Son of God because of His power over death exhibited by this fantastic miracle. Then, to illustrate the many difficulties associated with anything that Jesus revealed to the population of believers and hateful Jewish leaders, John also notes that the Jewish leaders were jealous, fearful, and plotted to kill Jesus after this very public resurrection. John 11: 46-53. Not only was Jesus targeted by these angry Jewish leaders, but Lazarus also became a marked man. Lazarus was becoming famous for being resurrected, and his very existence now served as a tangible, visible witness to the power and glory of Jesus. John 12: 9-11. The plight of Lazarus in being raised from the dead, and then being targeted for death again by the hypocritical Jewish leaders, is very ironic.

The joy of Mary and Martha at the return of their brother Lazarus from the dead is apparent in the story that follows in John. First, they held and hosted a great banquet to honor

THE GOD ORGASM

their Lord, with Lazarus and Jesus being the guests of honor. Mary worshipped and glorified Jesus by taking the time and effort and expense to anoint Him with very costly oil in the presence of the guests- the scene has always struck me as being very sensual in that the woman used her hair to do so. "Then Jesus six days before the passover came to Bethany, where Lazarus was, which had been dead, whom he raised from the dead. There they made him a supper; and Martha served: but Lazarus was one of them that sat at the table with him. Then took Mary a pound of ointment of spikenard, very costly, and anointed the feet of Jesus, and wiped his feet with her hair: and the house was filled with the odour of the ointment. Then saith one of his disciples, Judas Iscariot, Simon's son, which should betray him, Why was not this ointment sold for three hundred pence, and given to the poor? This he said, not that he cared for the poor; but because he was a thief, and had the bag, and bare what was put therein. Then said Jesus, Let her alone: against the day of my burying hath she kept this. For the poor always ye have with you; but me ye have not always. Much people of the Jews therefore knew that he was there: and they came not for Jesus' sake only, but that they might see Lazarus also, whom he had raised from the dead." John 12: 1-9.

As we will see in the next chapter, the death and resulting resurrection of Lazarus also triggered one of the most joyful and worshipful events in the Bible.

JOY FROM JESUS

As was mentioned in the previous Chapter, the joy and exhilaration and worshipful reactions to Jesus as a result of the curing of disease or the resurrection of the dead may not be great modern day examples of the joy that we should exhibit in worshipping our God and Jesus. As we have already said, it is very easy to be joyful when you are either cured of a lifelong, debilitating disease, or are suddenly alive after you have been declared to be very dead.

But, the Gospels are also replete with examples of how people found joy in worshipping Jesus in the more common and every day occurrences of their lives.

How did people in the New Testament during the time of Jesus find joy in their worship? In retrospect, it should not have been difficult to be joyful when the fulfillment of the promise of the Messiah was in your midst, but the trials of ministry, and the difficulties of life in general still had to be coped with by people. Couple that with the unbelief of many residents of Israel concerning the identity of Jesus, such as the Pharisees, Sadducees, and most of the ruling Sanhedrin of the Jews- the joy of having Jesus in their midst was totally lost on some people. It is easy for us to say in modern times that these people were ignorant fools. But, would you and I have also missed Jesus if He appeared to us in the United States in the twenty-first century for the first time, preached peace and love, and hung out with IRS agents, prostitutes, the homeless, and the sick (both mentally and physically)?

One of the best examples of the joy of worship, from a dual-sided perspective, is in the story of Jesus commissioning the seventy to go out into Israel and preach the good news and save souls. Luke 10. Luke sets the scene for the story very succinctly by simply stating, "After these things the LORD appointed other seventy also, and sent them two and two before his face into every city and place, whither he himself would come. Therefore said he unto them, The harvest truly is great, but the labourers are few: pray ye therefore the Lord of the harvest, that he would send forth labourers into his harvest." Luke 10: 1-2.

We don' know exactly what the commissioned disciples did in their sanctioned ministry, but Luke does tell us that, "the seventy returned again with joy, saying, Lord, even the devils are subject to us through thy name." Luke 10: 17. I find present in this short verse not only the joy of worship, but the sheer joy of serving others and ministering to other peoples' needs in the name of Jesus. The other great part of this story is the reaction of Jesus to the success and ministry of the people who he had sent out in His name. Jesus told them, "I beheld Satan as lightning fall from heaven." Luke 10: 18. More importantly, the satisfaction and pleasure of Jesus in seeing others serving in His name, and in the name of the Father, is very apparent at the conclusion of the story. "In that hour Jesus rejoiced in spirit, and said, I thank thee, O Father, Lord of heaven and earth, that thou hast hid these things from the wise and prudent, and hast revealed them unto babes: even so, Father; for so it seemed good in thy sight." Luke 10: 21. I love the imagery of our God who revels and finds pleasure in our successes and in the success of our service to others.

Yet another example of the presence of joy in worship in the Gospels during the life of Jesus is found in the many stories and parables of the exhilaration of successfully bringing the lost to a saving knowledge of the Lord Jesus Christ. Not only should there be personal joy in bringing the Gospel message of Jesus to those around us as a form of worship, but the following passages and parables make it clear that there is great joy in Heaven when someone accepts the Lord Jesus Christ as their Savior. Heaven as a joyful, final destination for believers should be an image that everyone enjoys partaking in.

"What man of you, having an hundred sheep, if he lose one of them, doth not leave the ninety and nine in the wilderness, and go after that which is lost, until he find it? And when he hath found it, he layeth it on his shoulders, rejoicing. And when he cometh home, he calleth together his friends and neighbours, saying unto them, Rejoice with me; for I have found my sheep which was lost. I say unto you, that likewise joy shall be in heaven over one sinner that repenteth, more than over ninety and nine just persons, which need no repentance. Either what woman having ten pieces of silver, if she lose one piece, doth not light a candle, and sweep the house, and seek diligently till she find it? And when she hath found it, she calleth her friends and her neighbours together, saying, Rejoice with me; for I have found the piece which I had lost. Likewise, I say unto you, there is joy in the presence of the angels of God over one sinner that repenteth." Luke 15: 4-10.

The story/parable of the Prodigal Son directly follows, and is very similar to the short parables of the redeemed sinner and the lost items found told by Jesus. But, the story is a more realistic example of a true, life situation which many people might encounter- I have always preferred to think of it as an actual, real-life story narrated to the audience by Jesus, and not a parable.

"And he said, A certain man had two sons: And the younger of them said to his father, Father, give me the portion of goods that falleth to me. And he divided unto them his living. And not many days after the younger son gathered all together, and took his journey into a far country, and there wasted his substance with riotous living. And when he had spent all, there arose a mighty famine in that land; and he began to be in want. And he went and joined himself to a citizen of that country; and he sent him into his fields to feed swine. And he would fain have filled his belly with the husks that the swine did eat: and no man gave unto him. And when he came to himself, he said, How many hired servants of my father's have bread enough and to spare, and I perish with hunger! I will arise and go to my father, and will say unto him, Father, I have sinned against heaven, and before thee, And am no more worthy to be called thy son: make me as one of thy hired servants. And he arose, and came to his father. But when he was yet a great way off, his father saw him, and had compassion, and ran, and fell on his neck, and kissed him. And the son said unto him, Father, I have sinned against heaven, and in thy sight, and am no more worthy to be called thy son. But the father said to his servants, Bring forth the best robe, and put it on him; and put a ring on his hand, and shoes on his feet: And bring hither the fatted calf, and kill it; and let us eat, and be merry: For this my son was dead, and is alive again; he was lost, and is found. And they began to be merry. Now his elder son was in the field: and as he came and drew nigh to the house, he heard musick and dancing. And he called one of the servants, and asked what these things meant. And he said unto him, Thy brother is come; and thy father hath killed the fatted calf, because he hath received him safe and sound. And he was angry, and would not go in: therefore came his father out, and intreated him. And he answering said to his father, Lo, these many years do I serve thee, neither transgressed I at any time thy commandment: and yet thou never gavest me a kid, that I might make merry with my friends: But as soon as this thy son was come, which hath devoured thy living with harlots, thou hast killed for him the fatted calf. And he said unto him, Son, thou art ever with me, and all that I have is thine. It was meet that we should make merry, and be glad: for this thy brother was dead, and is alive again; and was lost, and is found." Luke 15: 11-32.

The story of the Prodigal Son is an enhanced version of the stories of the lost items mentioned previously in Luke 15, as well as an allegory for the joy encountered in Heaven when the spiritually lost return and are found. But, it is also a tale of the element of forgiveness and putting aside personal disappointments and situations to find joy in our lives. The art of having joyful worship experiences in spite of personal circumstances can be discovered in the story of the Prodigal Son.

Of course, there is also a negative example of joylessness in the story of the Prodigal Son. The elder brother who had been dutiful and who consistently did his earthly father's bidding would not join in the joyful family party he came upon to celebrate his careless brother's return to the family. Selfishness, jealousy, and self-centeredness prevented this older brother from experiencing exhilaration at the return to the family fold of his wayward sibling, and the redemption of the younger man. How often do we as Christians fail to experience the joy of worshipping God in such a manner, as we get bogged down in personal troubles and trials which weeks or months later might well turn out to be unimportant and insignificant? In fact, finding joy in our worship of God is probably the outstanding distraction and panacea for any personal depression and funk we encounter in getting lost in the trials and problems of life.

THE GOD ORGASM

The sheer joy and exhilaration in worshipping and communing with Jesus is next found in the story of a man, most likely ostracized by Jewish society at the time because of his profession, but who was determined to see and meet the Lord in his actions and his deeds.

"And Jesus entered and passed through Jericho. And, behold, there was a man named Zacchaeus, which was the chief among the publicans, and he was rich. And he sought to see Jesus who he was; and could not for the press, because he was little of stature. And he ran before, and climbed up into a sycomore tree to see him: for he was to pass that way. And when Jesus came to the place, he looked up, and saw him, and said unto him, Zacchaeus, make haste, and come down; for to day I must abide at thy house. And he made haste, and came down, and received him joyfully. And when they saw it, they all murmured, saying, That he was gone to be guest with a man that is a sinner. And Zacchaeus stood, and said unto the Lord: Behold, Lord, the half of my goods I give to the poor; and if I have taken any thing from any man by false accusation, I restore him fourfold. And Jesus said unto him, This day is salvation come to this house, forsomuch as he also is a son of Abraham. For the Son of man is come to seek and to save that which was lost." Luke 19: 1-10.

The joy of Zacchaeus in seeing the Lord, and then having his zeal rewarded by Jesus when He came to his house to dine, resulted in the salvation of this tax collector and a life-changing reversal of attitude. Of course, the parallel between the story of Zacchaeus and the other tax collector in the Gospels, the Disciple Matthew, is very apparent also.

The joy of worshipping Jesus is also evident in three other passages of the Gospels, which involve different women, physical acts of worship, and rather startling scenes of sensual communion with our Lord. We have already mentioned the first of these incidents in the person of Mary, the sister of Lazarus.

"And one of the Pharisees desired him that he would eat with him. And he went into the Pharisee's house, and sat down to meat. And, behold, a woman in the city, which was a sinner, when she knew that Jesus sat at meat in the Pharisee's house, brought an alabaster box of ointment, And stood at his feet behind him weeping, and began to wash his feet with tears, and did wipe them with the hairs of her head, and kissed his feet, and anointed them with the ointment. Now when the Pharisee which had bidden him saw it, he spake within himself, saying, This man, if he were a prophet, would have known who and what manner of woman this is that toucheth him: for she is a sinner. And Jesus answering said unto him, Simon, I have somewhat to say unto thee. And he saith, Master, say on. There was a certain creditor which had two debtors: the one owed five hundred pence, and the other fifty. And when they had nothing to pay, he frankly forgave them both. Tell me therefore, which of them will love him most? Simon answered and said, I suppose that he, to whom he forgave most. And he said unto him, Thou hast rightly judged. And he turned to the woman, and said unto Simon, Seest thou this woman? I entered into thine house, thou gavest me no water for my feet: but she hath washed my feet with tears, and wiped them with the hairs of her head. Thou gavest me no kiss: but this woman since the time I came in hath not ceased to kiss my feet. My head with oil thou didst not anoint: but this woman hath anointed my feet with ointment. Wherefore I say unto thee, Her sins, which are many, are forgiven; for she loved much: but to whom little is forgiven, the same loveth little. And he said unto her, Thy sins are forgiven. And they that sat at meat with him began to say within themselves, Who is this that forgiveth sins also? And he said to the woman, Thy faith hath saved thee; go in peace." Luke 7: 36-50.

This scene is mind-blowing. This woman, described as a sinner (she was most likely a prostitute), spent a great deal of money acquiring oil with which to anoint the body of Jesus. The woman experienced the joy of worshipping our Lord by touching Him, caressing Him, and washing His feet off with her hair. It's not hard to imagine the indignant reaction of the Pharisee in questioning this very vivid scene of the physical worship of Jesus- Israeli men in the time of Jesus did not have public displays of affection with women, much less at the dining table. Foot washing itself was a common Oriental tradition of hospitality and politeness and manners, and necessity- the roads at the time were a dusty, dirty mess, and most travelers wore only open sandals when they walked. I have participated in foot washing in our more modern times in the three-part Communion service of the Grace Brethren Church, and the experience struck me as very intimate and very humbling. I don't think that I ever got used to it, and the symbolism in the modern service of Christ washing the feet of the Disciples was vividly brought to life during the ritual.

Jesus not only accepted the physical attention of this sinful woman (she needed a name), but used the entire scene as an object lesson for His Pharisee host, Simon, about both the forgiveness of sins, and the fact that He, as Messiah and God, could forgive sins. It's entirely possible that both lessons of Jesus were lost on Simon, the Pharisee.

The third instance of physical worship of Jesus by a woman is very similar to the others mentioned above. "After two days was the feast of the passover, and of unleavened bread: and the chief priests and the scribes sought how they might take him by craft, and put him to death. But they said, Not on the feast day, lest there be an uproar of the people. And being in Bethany in the house of Simon the leper, as he sat at meat, there came a woman having an alabaster box of ointment of spikenard very precious; and she brake the box, and poured it on his head. And there were some that had indignation within themselves, and said, Why was this waste of the ointment made? For it might have been sold for more than three hundred pence, and have been given to the poor. And they murmured against her. And Jesus said, Let her alone; why trouble ye her? she hath wrought a good work on me. For ye have the poor with you always, and whensoever ye will ye may do them good: but me ye have not always. She hath done what she could: she is come aforehand to anoint my body to the burying. Verily I say unto you, Wheresoever this gospel shall be preached throughout the whole world, this also that she hath done shall be spoken of for a memorial of her. Mark 14: 1-9.

Just as the other woman had done, this again unnamed woman took extremely expensive herbs and spices and used her hair to clean the feet of Jesus. The intimate nature of this same physical act of worship is very apparent if you attempt to visualize the scene. And, just like with the other events, at least one person was offended by the physical act of worship, and an alleged waste of money at the use of an extremely valuable commodity in this manner. The rebuke of those appalled by the use of the expensive herbs and spices for Jesus was again memorable, and an indication that the Lord gladly accepted and appreciated the physical worship and

THE GOD ORGASM

thanksgiving of this woman. As an aside here, before any theologians reading this send me an e-mail, there is some controversy over whether this incident related in Mark is really the same event of Mary (the sister of Lazarus) washing the feet of Jesus from Luke. While the location is correct in the version told in Mark, Bethany, the event narrated in Mark occurred during Holy Week right before the death of Jesus. The event in Luke occurred before Palm Sunday. Also, there is no Simon, the leper, in the story of Mary anointing Jesus in Luke, although some claim that he was the father of Lazarus.

Once again, while we will, unfortunately, never find joy on this earth in the desire to physically meet and greet Jesus, we should experience great joy in worshipping our God, meeting Him intimately by studying His word, and in prayer where we can talk to Him in person. And, the scenes of these women physically caring for and communing with Jesus just might be capable of being duplicated by us when we meet our Lord and Savior in Heaven (a topic we will examine later in this work).

Curiously, when I began my research for this book, I expected to find consistent elements of joy, gladness, and happiness in worship in one of the greatest and most important events in the history of our world- the Resurrection of our Lord Jesus Christ on the first Easter Sunday. But, my reading and research revealed very little stated joy in the return of Jesus to life on that glorious day. Exultation does not jump off the pages of any of the Gospels when the story of the Resurrection is narrated.

The verses which convey this mindset of joy at discovering that the Lord had arose from the dead are only found in less than a handful of places. In Matthew, Mary Magdalene and the other Mary, went to the tomb of Jesus bright and early on that first Easter morning in order to mourn (other passages in the Gospels say that they also intended to complete the preparation of His body, which was rushed because of the impending hour of the beginning of Passover on that Good Friday after the crucifixion).

"And, behold, there was a great earthquake: for the angel of the Lord descended from heaven, and came and rolled back the stone from the door, and sat upon it. His countenance was like lightning, and his raiment white as snow: And for fear of him the keepers did shake, and became as dead men. And the angel answered and said unto the women, Fear not ye: for I know that ye seek Jesus, which was crucified. He is not here: for he is risen, as he said. Come, see the place where the Lord lay. And go quickly, and tell his disciples that he is risen from the dead; and, behold, he goeth before you into Galilee; there shall ye see him: lo, I have told you. And they departed quickly from the sepulchre with fear and great joy; and did run to bring his disciples word. And as they went to tell his disciples, behold, Jesus met them, saying, All hail. And they came and held him by the feet, and worshipped him. Then said Jesus unto them, Be not afraid: go tell my brethren that they go into Galilee, and there shall they see me." Matthew 28: 2-10. In the passage, it is clearly stated that the women experienced "great joy," at what they discovered at the tomb, probably after their initial shock and fear had worn off.

Another narrative of the events immediately following the Resurrection, this time in Luke, tells the same story of the women visiting the tomb, the at-first veiled meeting of the risen Jesus with Cleopas and his wife on the road to Emmaus, and then the appearance of Jesus to the Disciples in the upper room. After each of these events, Luke simply and rather cryptically states the reaction of the Disciples- "they yet believed not for joy, and wondered." Luke 28: 41. The meaning of this phrase is very confusing. I believe it is stating that the joy of the followers of Jesus at the sudden appearance of the Lord was more muted because of their amazement and fear that He had returned to them. If that's the case, it's a rather stilted and strange way to phrase the emotions of the Disciples in the midst of a marvelous occurrence.

The final reference to the emotions of the Disciples at the Resurrection of Jesus is found in John, and most likely narrates the same events as described in the Luke passages referenced above. This time, John describes the reactions of the Disciples to the sudden appearance of the Resurrected Lord- "Then were the disciples glad, when they saw the Lord." John 20: 20. Once again, a feeling of "gladness" does not seem to do justice to the situation- I would much rather read that the Disciples of Jesus sang, danced, worshipped, and did cartwheels in the Upper Room at the appearance of their Lord, rather than just being "glad."

The seemingly almost stoic reaction of the Disciples to the physical proofs of the Resurrection of Jesus (the empty tomb, and the appearance of the Lord Himself to them), can perhaps be understood. All of these real time events in the space of time from Good Friday to Easter Sunday morning would have taken some time to ponder and digest properly.

The most fantastic example of joyful worship in the New Testament, and on a par with the revels of David in returning the Ark back to Jerusalem in the Old Testament, is the story of Palm Sunday. I have always loved the Palm Sunday story as an exceedingly joyful experience encountered during Holy Week, which always helps ease the temporarily tragic and mournful experience of the passion of our Lord which followed. My great appreciation of the Palm Sunday events was then magnified when I journeyed to the Holy Land in 2016 and had the privilege to descend the Mount of Olives and view the Garden of Gethsemane in person. Our tour bus parked somewhere near the peak of the Mount, and, after a brief history narrated by our excellent tour guide, we began descending to the valley below. I was so spiritually moved by my presence at this site in Israel that I lifted my voice in praise to God, and began shouting over and over, "Blessed is he who comes in the name of the Lord," and, "If these were to be silent, even the rocks would cry out." To my chagrin, no one else in our tour group of thirty some people joined my chants, and I felt more than a bit awkward shouting and carrying on when others were not doing the same. But, I abandoned my momentary sheepishness at my overt, vocal worship, and reveled in my own personal joy at celebrating Jesus in that manner. My walk down the Mount of Olives will always be treasured as a personal worship highlight in my spiritual life, mostly because of the joy I felt in following the footsteps of my Lord, and in recreating one of the most ecstatic scenes in Scriptures.

Once again, Luke contains my favorite rendition of the events of Palm Sunday. "And it came to pass, when he was come nigh to Bethphage and Bethany, at the mount called the mount of Olives, he sent two of his disciples, Saying, Go ye into the village over against you; in the which at your entering ye shall find a colt tied, whereon yet never man sat: loose him, and bring him hither. And if any man ask you, Why do ye loose him? thus shall ye say unto him, Because the Lord hath need of him. And they that were sent went their way, and found even as he had said unto them. And as they were loosing the colt, the owners thereof said unto them, Why loose ye the colt? And they said, The Lord hath need of him. And they brought him to Jesus: and they cast their garments upon the colt, and they set Jesus thereon. And as he went, they spread their clothes in the way. And when he was come nigh, even now at the descent of the mount of Olives, the whole multitude of the disciples began to rejoice and praise God with a loud voice for all the mighty works that they had seen; Saying, Blessed be the King that cometh in the name of the Lord: peace in heaven, and glory in the highest. And some of the Pharisees from among the multitude said unto him, Master, rebuke thy disciples. And he answered and said unto them, I tell you that, if these should hold their peace, the stones would immediately cry out." Luke 19: 29-40.

I always like to chuckle to myself (tongue-in-cheek) that the joyful events of Palm Sunday began with the theft of a colt by the disciples for Jesus to ride upon. Of course, more seriously, I presume that the use of the colt had been pre-arranged, or Jesus knew that the believing owners of the animals would immediately accept and understand the explanation that He told the disciples to give to the owners or their servants- if Jesus has need of my donkeys, take them.

The joy apparent on Palm Sunday has many nuances to it. It seems that the people who joyfully reveled in the presence of Jesus and worshipped Him on that day were inspired by several factors. First, the gospel of John explains that the entry into Jerusalem on Palm Sunday came soon after the raising of Lazarus from the dead, and the joyful feast in which Mary and Martha and Lazarus honored Jesus for performing that great service and miracle for their family. "Because that by reason of him (Lazarus) many of the Jews went away, and believed on Jesus. On the next day much people that were come to the feast, when they heard that Jesus was coming to Jerusalem, Took branches of palm trees, and went forth to meet him." John 12: 11-13.

As importantly though, the Jews, who were always proficient in their knowledge of the Torah, the histories, and the prophets, knew that an individual presenting Himself on a donkey, and riding in that manner into Jerusalem was performing an important symbolic act. Ever since the time of King David and King Solomon, riding a donkey in this manner into the Holy City was an overt claim to kingship over the nation of Israel.

"Then king David answered and said, Call me Bathsheba. And she came into the king's presence, and stood before the king. And the king sware, and said, As the LORD liveth, that hath redeemed my soul out of all distress, Even as I sware unto thee by the LORD God of Israel, saying, Assuredly Solomon thy son shall reign after me, and he shall sit upon my throne in my stead; even so will I certainly do this day. Then Bathsheba bowed with her face to the earth, and did reverence to the king, and said, Let my lord king David live for ever. And king David said, Call me Zadok the priest, and Nathan the prophet, and Benaiah the son of Jehoiada. And they came before the king. The king also said unto them, Take with you the servants of your lord, and cause Solomon my son to ride upon mine own mule, and bring him down to Gihon: And let Zadok the priest and Nathan the prophet anoint him there king over Israel: and blow ye with the trumpet, and say, God save king Solomon." I Kings 1: 28-34.

The additional symbolism of presenting a new King to the people on a donkey, instead of a horse, was intended to convey peace to the nation. Warriors and generals rode horses into war in the times of the Old Testament. A new ruler presenting himself on a donkey symbolized a pledge of a peaceful, tranquil rule. I always wonder if the symbolism was lost on the people of Israel in regard to Jesus, for many Jews in Israel were turned off and ultimately rejected Him when He came with His message of peace and salvation, rather than as a military Messiah who would remove the harsh Roman occupation of Israel.

The same Jews who recognized the symbolism of Jesus presenting Himself as a King to the nation while seated atop a donkey, in the tradition of David and Solomon, would also have recalled the words of the prophet Zechariah regarding a King presenting Himself to the nation of Israel.

"Rejoice greatly, O daughter of Zion; shout, O daughter of Jerusalem: behold, thy King cometh unto thee: he is just, and having salvation; lowly, and riding upon an ass, and upon a colt the foal of an ass. And I will cut off the chariot from Ephraim, and the horse from Jerusalem, and the battle bow shall be cut off: and he shall speak peace unto the heathen:

and his dominion shall be from sea even to sea, and from the river even to the ends of the earth." Zechariah 9: 9-10.

The prophecy of Zechariah, describing the events of Palm Sunday some 500 years before the time of Jesus, is amazing. As an aside, some commentators also use the Seventy Weeks of Daniel as one of the yardsticks to date the exact time of the entry of Jesus into Jerusalem on Palm Sunday. Daniel 9: 21-27.

In the Palm Sunday story, I find many different elements of worship that can instruct us in our more modern times. First there was action- the crowd in their joyful exultation over the presence of Jesus performed physical acts of worship. Clothes were spread on the path descending the Mount of Olives to form what would be the modern equivalent of a red carpet to welcome Jesus to Jerusalem. The Jewish crowds also moved and were physically active in their worship- they stripped or cut palm branches from the nearby trees to wave, so that they could revel in the presence of their Lord, Messiah, and longed for King. As I descended the Mount of Olives myself in the summer of 2016, my mind's eye could clearly envision the sea of palm branches being waved to honor and welcome Jesus as He rode down the hillside.

And, of course, there were words of praise shouted at Jesus as He descended the Mount of Olives. The Gospels don't convey the joy of the words entirely, but perhaps there was singing, loud chanting, and raucous Jewish rap as the crowd honored Jesus with its Hosannas, blessings, and joyful worship. The intensity of the verbal and audible worship was so great (both literally and figuratively) that it drove the always grouchy and complaining Pharisees to tell Jesus to, "rebuke thy disciples." Luke 19: 39. Jesus refused the request, and instead rebuked the whiners by stating, "I tell you that, if these should hold their peace, the stones would immediately cry out." Luke 19: 40.

If I could go back and be a witness to only two scenes of joyful worship in the Bible, I would choose to witness the entry of the Ark into Jerusalem when David danced before the Lord (II Samuel 6), and the events of Palm Sunday as narrated by the four Gospels. I will look forward to watching God's videos of those events when I get to Heaven.

JOY AFTER JESUS

After Jesus ascended to Heaven in the Gospels, the book of Acts continues with the stories of the Disciples and narrates the history of the early church. Acts itself describes the Ascension, which must have had a profound impact on the followers of Jesus. The restoration of Jesus to life after His crucifixion and death, and then the return of the Lord back to Heaven and His Father, certainly provided a vast array of emotions for the Disciples. There undoubtedly was joy at the Resurrection, and at the post-Resurrection appearances of Jesus to His followers, but it also must have been somewhat of a melancholy time when the realization hit the Disciples of Jesus that their Lord was now going to be absent from them for a long duration of time. The surge of the divergent emotions must have been difficult- a strong mix of both joy and sadness, stirred together with doses of melancholy at the overwhelming nature of everything which had occurred. But, as related in Acts, the reaction of the Disciples to the events and the departure of Jesus was to gird themselves for worship and spreading the Gospel as they all began new chapters in their spiritual journeys.

"And, being assembled together with them, commanded them that they should not depart from Jerusalem, but wait for the promise of the Father, which, saith he, ye have heard of me. For John truly baptized with water; but ye shall be baptized with the Holy Ghost not many days hence. When they therefore were come together, they asked of him, saying, Lord, wilt thou at this time restore again the kingdom to Israel? And he said unto them, It is not for you to know the times or the seasons, which the Father hath put in his own power. But ye shall receive power, after that the Holy Ghost is come upon you: and ye shall be witnesses unto me both in Jerusalem, and in all Judaea, and in Samaria, and unto the uttermost part of the earth. And when he had spoken these things, while they beheld, he was taken up; and a cloud received him out of their sight. And while they looked stedfastly toward heaven as he went up, behold, two men stood by them in white apparel; Which also said, Ye men of Galilee, why stand ye gazing up into heaven? this same Jesus, which is taken up from you into heaven, shall so come in like manner as ye have seen him go into heaven. Then returned they unto Jerusalem from the mount called Olivet, which is from Jerusalem a sabbath day's journey. And when they were come in, they went up into an upper room, where abode both Peter, and James, and John, and Andrew, Philip, and Thomas, Bartholomew, and Matthew, James the son of Alphaeus, and Simon Zelotes, and Judas the brother of James. These all continued with one accord in prayer and supplication, with the women, and Mary the mother of Jesus, and with his brethren." Act 1: 4-14.

The Disciples were no longer going to hide and quake in fear at what had happened to their Master, but they instead settled in to joyfully worship and serve their now departed Jesus Christ.

The story of the anointing of the Disciples by the Holy Spirit on Pentecost is one of the great narratives of the Bible, and I write this very close to the Sunday anniversary of when that occurred forty days after the first Easter Sunday. Once again, perhaps it was not difficult to decide to worship and follow Jesus after seeing men literally burning in zeal for the Lord (with their heads aflame, Acts 2: 3, followed by the ability of a diverse language crowd to understand and comprehend the great sermon of the Apostle Peter). Acts 2 very simply and succinctly states the reaction of the overwhelming numbers of the crowd. "Then they that gladly received his word were baptized: and the same day there were added unto them about three thousand souls." Acts 2: 41.

After the marvelous events of Pentecost, the Disciples and other followers of Jesus were undoubtedly fired up (pardon the pun) by what they had experienced and what they had accomplished for the Lord, and again were buttressed to joyfully worship and serve Jesus Christ. "And they, continuing daily with one accord in the temple, and breaking bread from house to house, did eat their meat with gladness and singleness of heart." Acts 2: 46.

Next in chronological order, there is another story of the joy and gladness apparent when a person was healed of a life-long infirmity and disability. Just as mentioned with the healing ministry of Jesus, it is understandably easy to rejoice and worship in such circumstances, but I love this story because when Peter and John invoked the power of Jesus to heal this particular individual, the man's reaction is priceless, and Acts describes one of the best celebrations of a recipient of a miracle.

"Now Peter and John went up together into the temple at the hour of prayer, being the ninth hour. And a certain man lame from his mother's womb was carried, whom they laid daily at the gate of the temple which is called Beautiful, to ask alms of them that entered into the temple; Who seeing Peter and John about to go into the temple asked an alms. And Peter, fastening his eyes upon him with John, said, Look on us. And he gave heed unto them, expecting to receive something of them. Then Peter said, Silver and gold have I none; but such as I have give I thee: In the name of Jesus Christ of Nazareth rise up and walk. And he took him by the right hand, and lifted him up: and immediately his feet and ankle bones received strength. And he leaping up stood, and walked, and entered with them into the temple, walking, and leaping, and praising God. And all the people saw him walking and praising God: And they knew that it was he which sat for alms at the Beautiful gate of the temple: and they were filled with wonder and amazement at that which had happened unto him." Acts 3: 1-10.

This man who was healed of his lameness must have skipped, danced, leaped for joy, shouted, and generally showed everyone around him that he was joyfully and enthusiastically worshipping God for his new gift of wholeness. The scene must have been amazing. The last verses of Acts relating his story state that he became a living witness, demonstrating to others the power and glory of God by his mere presence- most of the people who hung-out and frequented the Temple recognized the man as the crippled beggar who sat by the Beautiful gate. Acts 3: 10.

The book of Acts seems to be a never-ending calliope of examples of displaying joy and the power of worshipping our God in all situations, both good and bad. And, our next story is the best real-life example of this in the Bible. In this narrative, the Disciples preaching the Gospel message of Jesus, evidently were emphasizing the Resurrection of the Lord, and most likely once again pointed their fingers at the evil of the Jewish leaders in crucifying Him on the cross on that Good Friday. The Pharisees, Sadducees, scribes, and Sanhedrin quickly reached their tolerance point of this criticism, and took steps to silence the exuberance of the new Christian followers.

"And as they spake unto the people, the priests, and the captain of the temple, and the Sadducees, came upon them, Being grieved that they taught the people, and preached through Jesus the resurrection from the dead. And they laid hands on them, and put them in hold unto the next day: for it was now eventide. Howbeit many of them which heard the word believed; and the number of the men was about five thousand. And it came to pass on the morrow, that their rulers, and elders, and scribes, And Annas the high priest, and Caiaphas, and John, and Alexander, and as many as were of the kindred of the high priest, were gathered together at Jerusalem. And when they had set them in the midst, they asked, By what power, or by what name, have ye done this? Then Peter, filled with the Holy Ghost, said unto them, Ye rulers of the people, and elders of Israel, If we this day be examined of the good deed done to the impotent man, by what means he is made whole; Be it known unto you all, and to all the people of Israel, that by the name of Jesus Christ of Nazareth, whom ye crucified, whom God raised from the dead, even by him doth this man stand here before you whole. This is the stone which was set at nought of you builders, which is become the head of the corner. Neither is there salvation in any other: for there is none other name under heaven given among men, whereby we must be saved. Now when they saw the boldness of Peter and John, and perceived that they were unlearned and ignorant men, they marvelled; and they took knowledge of them, that they had been with Jesus. And beholding the man which was healed standing with them, they could say nothing against it. But when they had commanded them to go aside out of the council, they conferred among themselves, Saying, What shall we do to these men? for that indeed a notable miracle hath been done by them is manifest to all them that dwell in Jerusalem; and we cannot deny it. But that it spread no further among the people, let us straitly threaten them, that they speak henceforth to no man in this name. And they called them, and commanded them not to speak at all nor teach in the name of Jesus. But Peter and John answered and said unto them, Whether it be right in the sight of God to hearken unto you more than unto God, judge ye. For we cannot but speak the things which we have seen and heard. So when they had further threatened them, they let them go, finding nothing how they might punish them, because of the people: for all men glorified God for that which was done. For the man was above forty years old, on whom this miracle of healing was shewed. And being let go, they went to their own company, and reported all that the chief priests and elders had said unto them. And when they heard that, they lifted up their voice to God with one accord, and said, Lord, thou art God, which hast made heaven, and earth, and the sea, and all that in them is: Who by the mouth of thy servant David hast said, Why did the heathen rage, and the people imagine vain things? The kings of the earth stood up, and the rulers were gathered together against the Lord, and against his Christ. For of a truth against thy holy child Jesus, whom thou hast anointed, both Herod, and Pontius Pilate, with the Gentiles, and the people of Israel, were gathered together, For to do whatsoever thy hand and thy counsel determined before to be done. And now, Lord, behold their threatenings: and grant unto thy servants, that with all boldness they may speak thy word, By stretching forth thine hand to heal; and that signs and wonders may be done by the name of thy holy child Jesus. And when they had prayed, the place was shaken where they were assembled together; and they were all filled with the Holy Ghost, and they spake the word of God with boldness. And the multitude of them that believed were of one heart and of one soul: neither said any of them that ought of the things which he possessed was his own; but they had all things common." Act 4: 1-32.

I include these verses in their entirety because they are an excellent illustration of the determination to worship and obey God, and to evangelize, no matter what the circumstances and ill results may turn out to be.

After the first run-in and encounter with the Jewish leaders, the Disciples ignored the council's original orders to them, and continued to preach and teach about Jesus. Their return to action and their ministerial duties caused the leaders to once again have them brought in from the street for further threats and retribution. This time, the Disciples and followers of Jesus were not thrown into jail, but Acts instead narrates that they were physically punished with beatings. The description of the physical abuse is not given, but it is entirely possible that the beatings could have included the infamous thirty-nine strokes with the whip, which tore apart and mutilated skin. Thirty-nine strokes of the whip were the maximum limit allowed, because it was assumed by the Romans that forty strokes of the whip would kill.

After such physical punishment inflicted upon the followers of Jesus, Acts once again is very subtle and low-key when describing what occurred to these men, and their reactions to the beatings-"And to him they agreed: and when they had called the apostles, and beaten them, they commanded that they should not speak in the name of Jesus, and let them go. And they departed from the presence of the council, rejoicing that they were counted worthy to suffer shame for his name." Acts 5: 40-41. The Disciples of Jesus had come full circle from cowering in their upper room after the Crucifixion of the Lord to joyfully praising God that they were counted "worthy" to suffer shame and physical abuse for preaching and teaching about their Master. The story and the reactions each give me goosebumps whenever I read it.

I love to hear stories of successful evangelism, and to learn how my brothers and sisters in Christ came to know the Lord. In fact, my own story in that regard always strikes me as being rather dull. I am a Sunday-School-since-a-child Christian, whose parents (probably read my mom here) blessed me with an early introduction and belief in God and Jesus. Instead of my own story, I love lightning-bolt conversion stories, the stories of people who turn to a faith in Jesus as a result of a dire need or life crisis, as well as the stories of those sincere seekers of Jesus who finally come to the realization that becoming a Christ follower and believer is where they want to be.

The grand crescendo of these very different and very distinctive acceptance of Jesus stories by people I have both met and read about is the sheer joy and exultation which they experience when they finally know and accept the Lord, and invite Him into their lives. The best one of these stories is also in Acts, regarding a man foreign to Israel who was seeking, but who had not quite mentally decided to accept,

Jesus as his Lord and Savior, until he was assisted in his journey by the Apostle Philip.

"Then Philip went down to the city of Samaria, and preached Christ unto them. And the people with one accord gave heed unto those things which Philip spake, hearing and seeing the miracles which he did. For unclean spirits, crying with loud voice, came out of many that were possessed with them: and many taken with palsies, and that were lame, were healed. And there was great joy in that city." Acts 8: 5-8.

"And the angel of the Lord spake unto Philip, saying, Arise, and go toward the south unto the way that goeth down from Jerusalem unto Gaza, which is desert. And he arose and went: and, behold, a man of Ethiopia, an eunuch of great authority under Candace queen of the Ethiopians, who had the charge of all her treasure, and had come to Jerusalem for to worship, Was returning, and sitting in his chariot read Esaias the prophet. Then the Spirit said unto Philip, Go near, and join thyself to this chariot. And Philip ran thither to him, and heard him read the prophet Esaias, and said, Understandest thou what thou readest? And he said, How can I, except some man should guide me? And he desired Philip that he would come up and sit with him. The place of the scripture which he read was this, He was led as a sheep to the slaughter; and like a lamb dumb before his shearer, so opened he not his mouth: In his humiliation his judgment was taken away: and who shall declare his generation? for his life is taken from the earth. And the eunuch answered Philip, and said, I pray thee, of whom speaketh the prophet this? of himself, or of some other man? Then Philip opened his mouth, and began at the same scripture, and preached unto him Jesus. And as they went on their way, they came unto a certain water: and the eunuch said, See, here is water; what doth hinder me to be baptized? And Philip said, If thou believest with all thine heart, thou mayest. And he answered and said, I believe that Jesus Christ is the Son of God. And he commanded the chariot to stand still: and they went down both into the water, both Philip and the eunuch; and he baptized him. And when they were come up out of the water, the Spirit of the Lord caught away Philip, that the eunuch saw him no more: and he went on his way rejoicing. But Philip was found at Azotus: and passing through he preached in all the cities, till he came to Caesarea." Acts 8: 26-40.

THE GOD ORGASM

I have always assumed in this story that this Egyptian eunuch was a believing Jew at the time, or at least a God follower who realized that he worshipped the same God of the Jews. He had just left the Temple in Jerusalem after expending a great deal of time and energy to travel there and worship God. But, it is obvious from the circumstances of the story that the eunuch had absolutely no idea how Jesus fit into his God-belief mindset. In fact, it's not clear from the Acts narrative that the eunuch had even heard about Jesus and His mission and sacrifice at that time. The eunuch, most importantly, was on the mind of Jesus (stated by invoking the often-used term Angel of the Lord), and He dispatched Philip to personally talk to and teach this man. Philip came upon the eunuch, and, not coincidentally, the man was reading a Messianic prophecy and description from the prophet Isaiah comparing the Messiah to a lamb being led to slaughter. Philip explained this important Old Testament passage to the eunuch, taught him the Gospel of Jesus as the Crucified lamb and Messiah, and the man believed. Not only did the man believe, but the now teacher and student found a watering hole out in the wilds of the Gaza desert, and Philip immediately baptized the eunuch on the spot.

One of my favorite parts of this narrative is the revelation of the general truth about evangelism, and our mission in talking to people, even if we see no immediate results from our own efforts, and leave the harvest to the continuing follow-up efforts of others. When Philip first came upon the eunuch, and observed that he was at least seeking to such a level that he was reading the scrolls of Isaiah (and the appropriate Messianic passage), he inquired as to whether the man knew the meaning and importance of what he was reading and studying. The eunuch honestly responded, "How can I, except some man should guide me?" Act 8: 31. The simple and earnest response of the eunuch to Philip's question should be our key goal in talking to people about Jesus and the Gospel. There are many, many inquiring minds seeking God out there, who would be receptive to the Gospel message if we would only take the time to boldly explain the message of Jesus to them. In my experience, for every hostile person who is not receptive to the Gospel or any evangelistic efforts, there are twice as many people who would listen to your message, or who are at some early to midway point of seriously considering the impact of God and Jesus, and inviting them into their lives.

The culmination of this story is the greatest part of it. The Ethiopian eunuch went back to his country and his foreign land "rejoicing" in his new faith and his new knowledge of the Lord Jesus Christ. Acts 8: 39. And, I have always imagined as a postscript to the story that this person, who had an influential position in the Ethiopian royal court, returned to the palace of Candace and to his fellow countrymen, and told them about the joy of the Gospel of Jesus as well. What a great story in our Bible.

The later chapters of Acts chronicle Paul and his fellow workers for the Lord, and, unfortunately, they encounter strife, divisions, resistance, and persecutions which should have all combined to rob them of their joyful worship of God. "And the next sabbath day came almost the whole city together to hear the word of God. But when the Jews saw the multitudes, they were filled with envy, and spake against those things which were spoken by Paul, contradicting and blaspheming. Then Paul and Barnabas waxed bold, and said,

It was necessary that the word of God should first have been spoken to you: but seeing ye put it from you, and judge yourselves unworthy of everlasting life, lo, we turn to the Gentiles. For so hath the Lord commanded us, saying, I have set thee to be a light of the Gentiles, that thou shouldest be for salvation unto the ends of the earth. And when the Gentiles heard this, they were glad, and glorified the word of the Lord: and as many as were ordained to eternal life believed. And the word of the Lord was published throughout all the region." Acts 13: 44-49. The act of gladly receiving the word of God and worshipping Him should not be limited to the first time that we accept God into our lives, and Jesus as our Savior, but for every day and moment as we worship Him and live in His word.

Our next example of joyful worship from Acts has some negative ramifications to it. It begins by taking note of the joy which was apparent to both the new Gentile converts, as well as the followers of Jesus, that the non-Jews had been accepted into the baptism of the Holy Spirit and the family of God. But, the situation then turned sour when certain legalistic Jews, those of the sect of the Pharisees (of course), were not happy that it was so easy for the Gentiles to join the group of believers. It was as if the old boys club resented and were jealous of the lack of an initiation and waiting period for the new people who wanted to follow Jesus. These Pharisees demanded that the Old Testament law of Moses be strictly followed, and that all the new Gentile converts had to be circumcised to signify their acceptance of the covenant with God.

"And certain men which came down from Judaea taught the brethren, and said, Except ye be circumcised after the manner of Moses, ye cannot be saved. When therefore Paul and Barnabas had no small dissension and disputation with them, they determined that Paul and Barnabas, and certain other of them, should go up to Jerusalem unto the apostles and elders about this question. And being brought on their way by the church, they passed through Phenice and Samaria, declaring the conversion of the Gentiles: and they caused great joy unto all the brethren. And when they were come to Jerusalem, they were received of the church, and of the apostles and elders, and they declared all things that God had done with them. But there rose up certain of the sect of the

Pharisees which believed, saying, That it was needful to circumcise them, and to command them to keep the law of Moses. And the apostles and elders came together for to consider of this matter. And when there had been much disputing, Peter rose up, and said unto them, Men and brethren, ye know how that a good while ago God made choice among us, that the Gentiles by my mouth should hear the word of the gospel, and believe. And God, which knoweth the hearts, bare them witness, giving them the Holy Ghost, even as he did unto us; And put no difference between us and them, purifying their hearts by faith. Now therefore why tempt ye God, to put a yoke upon the neck of the disciples, which neither our fathers nor we were able to bear? But we believe that through the grace of the LORD Jesus Christ we shall be saved, even as they. Then all the multitude kept silence, and gave audience to Barnabas and Paul, declaring what miracles and wonders God had wrought among the Gentiles by them. And after they had held their peace, James answered, saying, Men and brethren, hearken unto me: Simeon hath declared how God at the first did visit the Gentiles, to take out of them a people for his name. And

THE GOD ORGASM

to this agree the words of the prophets; as it is written, After this I will return, and will build again the tabernacle of David, which is fallen down; and I will build again the ruins thereof, and I will set it up: That the residue of men might seek after the Lord, and all the Gentiles, upon whom my name is called, saith the Lord, who doeth all these things. Known unto God are all his works from the beginning of the world. Wherefore my sentence is, that we trouble not them, which from among the Gentiles are turned to God: But that we write unto them, that they abstain from pollutions of idols, and from fornication, and from things strangled, and from blood. For Moses of old time hath in every city them that preach him, being read in the synagogues every sabbath day. Then pleased it the apostles and elders with the whole church, to send chosen men of their own company to Antioch with Paul and Barnabas; namely, Judas surnamed Barsabas and Silas, chief men among the brethren, And they wrote letters by them after this manner; The apostles and elders and brethren send greeting unto the brethren which are of the Gentiles in Antioch and Syria and Cilicia. Forasmuch as we have heard, that certain which went out from us have troubled you with words, subverting your souls, saying, Ye must be circumcised, and keep the law: to whom we gave no such commandment: It seemed good unto us, being assembled with one accord, to send chosen men unto you with our beloved Barnabas and Paul, Men that have hazarded their lives for the name of our Lord Jesus Christ. We have sent therefore Judas and Silas, who shall also tell you the same things by mouth. For it seemed good to the Holy Ghost, and to us, to lay upon you no greater burden than these necessary things; That ye abstain from meats offered to idols, and from blood, and from things strangled, and from fornication: from which if ye keep yourselves, ye shall do well. Fare ye well. So when they were dismissed, they came to Antioch: and when they had gathered the multitude together, they delivered the epistle: Which when they had read, they rejoiced for the consolation." Acts 15: 1-31.

Cooler and more logical heads finally prevailed concerning this dispute of faith about circumcision, and Paul and the others in the council of Jerusalem determined to keep the Gentiles zealous in their faith and their new-found beliefs in the Lord Jesus Christ, rather than being distracted and hung-

THE GOD ORGASM

up as to whether the men had to be circumcised to join the club. Faith won out over legalism, and there was joy over the decision so that the real work of worshipping God and serving Him could still take place.

Our penultimate example from Acts about the joy of having God and Jesus in our lives arose yet again when Paul and his assistants faced persecution and adversity. In this situation, Paul's adversaries rose up when he removed a demon from a soothsaying woman who was making great financial gain for her handlers/owners because of the fees they charged the people to hear her predictions. The turmoil and near riot which resulted from this conflict led to Paul being thrown into jail yet again.

"And when her masters saw that the hope of their gains was gone, they caught Paul and Silas, and drew them into the marketplace unto the rulers, And brought them to the magistrates, saying, These men, being Jews, do exceedingly trouble our city, And teach customs, which are not lawful for us to receive, neither to observe, being Romans. And the multitude rose up together against them: and the magistrates rent off their clothes, and commanded to beat them. And when they had laid many stripes upon them, they cast them into prison, charging the jailor to keep them safely: Who, having received such a charge, thrust them into the inner prison, and made their feet fast in the stocks." Acts 16: 19-24.

Since God often arranges and works for His good and His plan in such circumstances, an amazing event then occurred which turned into a life-altering and soul-altering event for Paul's jailer, his family, and his entire household. "And at midnight Paul and Silas prayed, and sang praises unto God: and the prisoners heard them. And suddenly there was a great earthquake, so that the foundations of the prison were shaken: and immediately all the doors were opened, and every one's bands were loosed. And the keeper of the prison awaking out of his sleep, and seeing the prison doors open, he drew out his sword, and would have killed himself, supposing that the prisoners had been fled. But Paul cried with a loud voice, saying, Do thyself no harm: for we are all here. Then he called for a light, and sprang in, and came trembling, and fell down before Paul and Silas, And brought them out, and said, Sirs, what must I do to be saved? And they said, Believe on the

THE GOD ORGASM

Lord Jesus Christ, and thou shalt be saved, and thy house. And they spake unto him the word of the Lord, and to all that were in his house. And he took them the same hour of the night, and washed their stripes; and was baptized, he and all his, straightway. And when he had brought them into his house, he set meat before them, and rejoiced, believing in God with all his house. Acts 16: 25-34.

This jailer evidently, under the local laws and Roman laws of the time, could have been executed for dereliction of duty when the earthquake threw open the prison doors and created a means and method for Paul and Silas and the other prisoners to flee their captivity. Thankfully, Paul's first impulse (perhaps both knowing the law and the jailer's duties, and heeding the instructions of the Holy Spirit) was not to flee from the unpleasant conditions, but to assure the jailer that they were still all present and accounted for. And, Paul instead chose to minister to the spiritual condition of the jailer and to tell him about Jesus and the Cross. When the jailer and the members of his household were baptized and accepted Jesus, the verse in Acts simply relates that they "rejoiced." Acts 16: 34.

Our last example from Acts again illustrates Paul in a very dire situation, persecuted, and held in prison (the man may have been comfortable by that time in those straits- he was incarcerated very many times). Beginning in Acts 21, Paul traveled to Jerusalem, forewarned by the prophecy of Agabus (Acts 21: 10-11), that his presence in the Holy City would lead to his incarceration. Paul's fame was so broad and well known at the time that he entered the Temple and a near riot ensued. The Apostle was taken into custody, faced the Sanhedrin and the same Ananias who had Crucified his Lord, and was the subject of a plot by his enemies to kill him. The Roman soldier in charge of the prison learned of the plan to kill Paul and determined to secretly send him to Felix, the Roman governor, who resided at maritime Caesaria. Felix was well aware of the Jewish customs of the inhabitants of his region, and Paul seemed joyful to be able to defend himself and his Christian religion to the Roman governor. "Then Paul, after that the governor had beckoned unto him to speak, answered, Forasmuch as I know that thou hast been of many years a judge unto this nation, I do the more cheerfully answer for myself." Acts 24: 12. Felix let Paul simmer in prison, until he

THE GOD ORGASM

was succeeded by Festus, and then Roman king Agrippa visited Festus in Caesaria. Paul was then given an audience before Agrippa.

"Then Agrippa said unto Paul, Thou art permitted to speak for thyself. Then Paul stretched forth the hand, and answered for himself: I think myself happy, king Agrippa, because I shall answer for myself this day before thee touching all the things whereof I am accused of the Jews: Especially because I know thee to be expert in all customs and questions which are among the Jews: wherefore I beseech thee to hear me patiently. My manner of life from my youth, which was at the first among mine own nation at Jerusalem, know all the Jews; Which knew me from the beginning, if they would testify, that after the most straitest sect of our religion I lived a Pharisee. And now I stand and am judged for the hope of the promise made of God, unto our fathers: Unto which promise our twelve tribes, instantly serving God day and night, hope to come. For which hope's sake, king Agrippa, I am accused of the Jews. Why should it be thought a thing incredible with you, that God should raise the dead?" Acts 26: 1-8. Notice that this time Paul was "happy" to be able to speak of the

Gospel of Jesus Christ before yet another high Roman official. Paul's praise and worship of the Lord continued joyfully even though he was a prisoner and denied his liberty.

I was fortunate enough to visit maritime Caesaria in the summer of 2016 on my tour of the Holy Land. The site was full of fascinating things to see- Roman viaducts still standing, the ruins of ancient buildings, and even a chariot racing track. For our purposes here, a large amphitheater at the location of Paul's defense has been reconstructed, and the antiquities experts researched, recreated, and marked the spot where Paul gave his famous defenses of the faith to Festus and Agrippa. I believe that part of the original stadium still stood at this specific location, or was restored to it. It gave me goose bumps to know that I got to stand at the exact spot where the Apostle Paul had zealously and eloquently and joyfully orated about his faith in Jesus Christ and the Gospel.

THE GOD ORGASM

GOD'S GIFT OF JOY- SEX

The joy which should be found in worshipping God has other parallels and examples in the pages of the Bible. And, sensory joy, satisfaction, exultation, and euphoria are quite often found in another topic of the Bible that we are now going to tie in with worship. We are now going to explore what the joy of worship has to do with sex and human sexuality.

Whatever concept of God that you are beginning reading this book with, the one undeniable truth about God is that God must love sex and the sexual nature of our lives, and perhaps even the sexual nature of His own existence. Because, the Bible is replete with references to sex, sensuality, and the sex drives and lives of the characters of the Bible. Why does a book such as the Bible have so many references to, and allusions to, and stories about sex? Perhaps because

God finds great joy and revelry in the act of sex between human beings, and because it is certainly a gift given by God to all of us. We will expand on that theme and explanation as we move along in this work.

Even the story of the creation of Adam and Eve, and what happened thereafter in the lives of the citizens of the Old Testament of the Bible, can be used to demonstrate the sexuality and sensuality of God. For example, when Adam told God that he was lonely, and wanted a help mate, God was quick to know what to do on his behalf in the creation story.

"And out of the ground the LORD God formed every beast of the field, and every fowl of the air; and brought them unto Adam to see what he would call them: and whatsoever Adam called every living creature, that was the name thereof. "And Adam gave names to all cattle, and to the fowl of the air, and to every beast of the field; but for Adam there was not found an help meet for him. And the LORD God caused a deep sleep to fall upon Adam, and he slept: and he took one of his ribs, and closed up the flesh instead thereof; And the rib, which the LORD God had taken from man, made he a woman, and brought her unto the man. And Adam said, This is now bone of my bones, and flesh of my flesh: she shall be called Woman, because she was taken out of Man. Therefore shall a man leave his father and his mother, and shall cleave unto his wife: and they shall be one flesh. And they were both naked, the man and his wife, and were not ashamed." Genesis 2: 19-25. I am an avid reader and studier of my Bible, and many times there is a great annoyance when I do so at what I somewhat jocularly call the unanswered questions of Scripture. One of these very early questions is exactly where God found or invented the idea of different sexes for man. Obviously, the concept existed first for animals, because I assume each species needed to have a way to reproduce and continue its kind. But, it is also a Biblical theological assumption that when God created man His intentions always were that man was going to live forever. One of the punishments meted out by God as a result of the acts of Adam and Eve in eating the forbidden fruit was that they would die and return to the earth from where they arose. "In the sweat of thy face shalt thou eat bread, till thou return unto the ground; for out of it wast thou taken: for dust thou art, and unto dust shalt thou return." Genesis 3: 9.

Everlasting people don't need to reproduce themselves, or at least I have always considered that it would be a problem if they did, for the planet would soon be overtaxed and overburdened by having to find room for all of those citizens who never would die. As a result, why did God invent and create the female of the human species? The concept of male and female must have already existed in the experiences and mind of God. Were there female sexed individuals in Heaven, for example? Were the angels, perhaps, created with more than one sex existing in their kind, both male and female? I again think that a logical assumption is that long before the creation of man and woman on the Earth that God had already invented the concept of sexual differences, and the fact that there would be a male and a female of any species with very different body parts and functions.

In the first Chapter of Genesis it is quite emphatically stated that the man and woman were created in the image of God. "And God said, Let us make man in our image, after our likeness: and let them have dominion over the fish of the sea, and over the fowl of the air, and over the cattle, and over all the earth, and over every creeping thing that creepeth upon the earth. So God created man in his own image, in the image of God created he him; male and female created he them." Genesis 1: 26-27. To further explore my theory that different sexes somehow existed in Heaven, the verses above are very emphatic that both man and woman were each created in the image of God. As a result, it is quite apparent to me that there is something about God, or some quality of God, which is both male and female in either appearance, mindset, or both. No, I am not saying that God, Jesus, and the Trinity are either plurally, or singularly, strictly female in any composition that man can understand. But, the feminine nature of God is worthy of at least an inquiry from the finite minds of human beings.

And, no, in our modern, politically correct world, I am definitely not suggesting that God is some kind of gender confused, multi-sexual being. I sincerely doubt whether God requires any kind of abstract sexual identity as human beings recognize the term. But, if God wished to do that and to be that way, I could readily digest and accept that fact. Once again, it's the potter and the clay metaphor- the Creator can do what He wants to do, but we don't have the option to be anything but what God created us to be, distinctly male or distinctly female.

The second important point of the creation of Adam and Eve for my purposes is that the first couple were "both naked, the man and his wife, and were not ashamed." Genesis 2: 25. The obvious companion train of thought to that verse is that God also did not mind that Adam and Eve were naked, or He would have told them quite bluntly and quickly to put some clothes on. God obviously enjoyed the view of the naked human body as He conversed with the first couple when He visited them in the Garden of Eden. I totally agree- the naked human body is certainly very wonderfully, artfully, and beautifully made, especially because Adam and Eve were probably very fit individuals who were never subjected to bad or unhealthy food and unhealthy environmental conditions. God could enjoy viewing the beauty of His creation, and He most likely did so.

Then, after Adam and Eve were expelled from the Garden of Eden as a result of their sin, they reproduced very quickly and bore their first sons, Abel and Cain. "And Adam knew Eve his wife; and she conceived, and bare Cain, and said, I have gotten a man from the LORD. And she again bare his brother Abel. And Abel was a keeper of sheep, but Cain was a tiller of the ground." Genesis 4: 1-2. The story of the appearance of children to Adam and Eve brings up another one of my Biblical questions which has no good answer. That question is- how did Adam and Eve learn about the acts necessary to have sex? Did God instruct them on how to use their bodies? It's not so far-fetched to imagine that occurred. Did God actually leave an instructional manual for these two earthly pioneers- a sort of Everything You Always Wanted to Know About Sex? Or, were the sex acts and how to act sexually ingrained in the genetic code and instincts of both Adam and Eve? Any of those options are plausible.

After the story of Adam and Eve and their progeny unfolds, along with telling the history of the people who followed them in the first line of human beings, a strange tale of people called the "sons of God" unfolds in the pages of Genesis. "And it came to pass, when men began to multiply on the face of the earth, and daughters were born unto them,

That the sons of God saw the daughters of men that they were fair; and they took them wives of all which they chose. And the LORD said, My spirit shall not always strive with man, for that he also is flesh: yet his days shall be an hundred and twenty years. There were giants in the earth in those days; and also after that, when the sons of God came in unto the daughters of men, and they bare children to them, the same became mighty men which were of old, men of renown. And God saw that the wickedness of man was great in the earth, and that every imagination of the thoughts of his heart was only evil continually." Genesis 6: 1-5. Theologians are split as to who these "sons of God" mentioned above were. At least one train of thought has studied and analyzed these verses and has concluded that residents of Heaven may have come down to earth to have sex with and to reproduce with female human beings. Other theologians just state that the "sons of God" were the mighty warriors and rulers of the earth at that time. Whatever analysis is indeed true, the problem in my mind is why these few verses are even included in Genesis 6. I say that because immediately following those verses Noah is introduced, and the ark was built and the great flood occurred. Whatever entities or beings, mere men or Heavenly beings, were the fathers of these children, they did not survive the great flood unless they ended up being the children of Noah in some form or capacity.

Since this is very much another of my unknown mysteries of the Bible, let's consider for a moment an idea that the Sons of God were actually residents of Heaven. If so, is it true that God and His creations living in Heaven can come to the earth and have sex and procreate with human beings? We will never know the real answer to that question, but I do know that in my Bible it occurred just that way at least once in the form of the Son of God.

The sex lives, and sex antics, of the characters of the Old Testament then continued with Abraham, Jacob and his sons, King David, and King Solomon.

ABRAHAM, JACOB AND PROGENY, DAVID, SOLOMON

The following chapters of this book will postulate that the act of having sex is a form of joyful worship to God, as well as a prophetic metaphor of the future. Accept that as true for a moment, and then consider the examples of the sex lives of

Biblical characters portrayed in the Old Testament. For the most part, the history of the sexual nature of the lives of the Patriarchs was just plain awful, with a few exceptions.

Beginning with Abraham in Genesis 15, God promised that his seed would be given the land of Israel. But, at the time of God's promise, Abraham did not have any natural children. Rather than wait on the promises of God to unfold in God's time, as soon as the next chapter of Genesis Abraham, and Sarah, his wife, took matters into their own hands (at the suggestion of Sarah), and Abraham instead had sex with, and impregnated their slave girl, Hagar. Genesis 16. The lurid nature of this story is neither obedient, or worshipful, to God, and it is perhaps the first of many examples that human beings can and will misuse God's intentions for sex.

Jacob, the grandson of Abraham, later began his own chronicle of the misuse of sex, by having multiple partners and wives and concubines which he employed for that purpose. First in time, Jacob ended up marrying the sisters Rachel and Leah. Genesis 29. When the sister wives had periodic bouts of infertility, Jacob then emulated his grandfather's behavior by having sexual relations with the slave staff when he had children with first Bilhah, and then Zilpah. Genesis 30. Jacob, the progenitor of the twelve tribes of Israel, created a situation where his sons, who would be the founders of each tribe, had four different mothers and four different backgrounds. You literally need to have a flow chart and huge family tree outline to recall which of the wives or concubines fathered each of Jacob's children (he had one daughter also).

In a not so great example of a son emulating the sexual behavior of his father, Judah (yes, a member of the genetic line of Jesus as the forefather of both Mary and Joseph), ended up having sex with his daughter-in-law, Tamar, after his son who had wed Tamar died. Genesis 38.

I often ask myself what in the world was the purpose of having these lurid stories about the misuse of sex in the pages of the Old Testament? I suppose that they are included partly because they provide a story of the biographies and histories of the patriarchs. The relationships, even though greatly tangled, demonstrate the family trees of the founders of Israel.

But, I long ago concluded that the examples of negative sexual antics depicted in Genesis are also there as a warning and a lesson- a type of moral stating that these people didn't follow the wishes and desires of God as to sex, greatly erred, and complicated their lives because of their multiple sex partners, and multiple wives. Of course, their bad behaviors also complicated the lives of their children and future generations.

The negative examples of sexual behavior in the characters of the Bible continue with the stories of King David and his son, King Solomon. The favor David found in the eyes of God, and his generally exemplary behaviors and worship habits, are stained by the narrative of his sexual antics and sins with the voluptuous and charming Bathsheba. "And it came to pass, after the year was expired, at the time when kings go forth to battle, that David sent Joab, and his servants with him, and all Israel; and they destroyed the children of Ammon, and besieged Rabbah. But David tarried still at Jerusalem. And it came to pass in an eveningtide, that David arose from off his bed, and walked upon the roof of the king's house: and from the roof he saw a woman washing herself; and the woman was very beautiful to look upon. And David sent and enquired after the woman. And one said, Is not this

Bathsheba, the daughter of Eliam, the wife of Uriah the Hittite? And David sent messengers, and took her; and she came in unto him, and he lay with her; for she was purified from her uncleanness: and she returned unto her house. And the woman conceived, and sent and told David, and said, I am with child." II Samuel 11: 1-5. The sudden pregnancy of Bathsheba, and the dilemmas that David found himself in as a result of his sexual fling, then became a soap opera like story of lies, deception, and even the murder of Bathsheba's husband, Uriah, upon the command of David. II Samuel 11 and 12.

David's sexual sins and his sin of murder were personally costly and swiftly punished by God. God forbade David from his desire to build a permanent structure for the worship of his beloved God. And, tragically, the child born of the liaison between David and Bathsheba was stricken dead by God as well. II Samuel 12. The tragic death of this child is yet another great example in the Bible that sexual sins have far greater ramifications and results than just the effects upon the two people involved in the intimate relationship.

David's other son with Bathsheba, King Solomon, is depicted as a very interesting character. Solomon asked for wisdom from God, was granted his request, and became renowned as the wisest man in the world. He was also deemed to be the richest man in the world as well. God did permit Solomon to build the Temple which would permanently house the Jewish worship of God. The story of Solomon and the Queen of Sheba is very interesting, and almost seems sensual without being overtly sexual at the conversation and meeting between the two earthly rulers. But, once again, Solomon's reputation is seen as damaged in the pages of the Bible because of his sexual cravings and misbehaviors. I Kings 11: 3 informs us, "And he had seven hundred wives, princesses, and three hundred concubines: and his wives turned away his heart."

My ever pondering mind has often thought that it may have actually been fun to be a wife or concubine to King Solomon. There were so many of them that the King would not have time to be demanding as to any individual woman, and they probably were all treated very royally.

THE GOD ORGASM

In any event, the final analysis of the life of King Solomon was that his many wives and concubines turned his heart away from God. The sad demise of Solomon in the last verses of I Kings 11 blames this on the wives causing him to worship other gods. The melancholy conclusion of the life of Solomon was said to be, "And Solomon did evil in the sight of the Lord, and went not fully after the Lord, as did David his father." I Kings 11: 6.

But, there are more positive examples of pure sexual behavior in the pages of Genesis, and they do serve to illustrate God's gift of sex to us as a joyful form of worship and obedience to Him. First, and it is rather subtly understated in the pages of the Bible, Isaac serves as an example of how to be a sexually faithful husband and father. Rebekah married Isaac, sight unseen, after Abraham's servant was sent to find Isaac a wife among Abraham's next of kin. Genesis 24. The servant asked Rebekah to come with him and to be a wife to a man she had never met. In Genesis 35, the twins Jacob and Esau were born, and the story of Rebekah and Isaac then quickly became one of favoritism by each parent for a different son, and the ensuing sibling rivalry and conflict between the boys. The death of Isaac is reported at the end of Genesis 35: 28-29. Throughout the biography and life story of Isaac, there is no report in our Bible that he married multiple wives, or was ever unfaithful to Rebekah, or that he acted out sexually (some Bible commentators claim that Isaac had a second wife, but I find no proof of that in Genesis).

In regard to the patriarchs, there is, of course, one outstanding example of sexual purity in the circumstance of great temptation not to be so chaste.

In Genesis 39, the rather lurid tale of the attempt to seduce Joseph, one of the sons of Jacob, by Potiphar's wife is told. Joseph was sold into slavery by his jealous brothers, and ended up in Egypt working for one of the Pharaoh's chief officials, Potiphar. Potiphar liked and respected Joseph, and he put him in charge of his entire household. God certainly provided for Joseph in the midst of his bad situation after being betrayed and hated by his brothers.

But, the idyllic work situation of Joseph was ruined because the wife of his employer lusted after him and tried to seduce him. In Genesis 39: 7, the beginning of this story of sex and steamy seduction bluntly says that, "his master's wife cast her eyes upon Joseph, and she said Lie with me." The woman is never given a name in the story, so we'll call her Mrs. Potiphar here- some of these women in stories in the Bible beg for a name.

Joseph refused to have sex with Mrs. Potiphar that first time, and the attempts at seduction continued several times after that. The last refusal of Joseph to have sex with Mrs. Potiphar resulted in her telling her husband a huge lie that Joseph tried to assault her. "And it came to pass, as she spake to Joseph day by day, that he hearkened not unto her, to lie by her, or to be with her. And it came to pass about this time, that Joseph went into the house to do his business; and there was none of the men of the house there within. And she caught him by his garment, saying, Lie with me: and he left his garment in her hand, and fled, and got him out. And it came to pass, when she saw that he had left his garment in her hand, and was fled forth, That she called unto the men of her house, and spake unto them, saying, See, he hath brought in an Hebrew unto us to mock us; he came in unto me to lie with me, and I cried with a loud voice: And it came to pass, when he heard that I lifted up my voice and cried, that he left his garment with me, and fled, and got him out. And she laid up his garment by her, until his lord came home. And she spake unto him according to these words, saying, The Hebrew servant, which thou hast brought unto us, came in unto me to mock me: And it came to pass, as I lifted up my voice and cried, that he left his garment with me, and fled out. And it came to pass, when his master heard the words of his wife, which she spake unto him, saying, After this manner did thy servant to me; that his wrath was kindled. And Joseph's master took him, and put him into the prison, a place where the king's prisoners were bound: and he was there in the prison. But the LORD was with Joseph, and shewed him mercy, and gave him favour in the sight of the keeper of the prison. And the keeper of the prison committed to Joseph's hand all the prisoners that were in the prison; and whatsoever they did there, he was the doer of it." Genesis 39: 10-22. The ethical and moral decision of Joseph to follow the word of God as to sex, and then being unceremoniously tossed into prison as a result, is a great example of the old saying "no good deed goes unpunished." Poor Joseph.

THE GOD ORGASM

The reason for Joseph's decision to remain sexually chaste and pure is clearly set forth in this story in the verse preceding the above quoted sections. "There is none greater in this house than I; neither hath he kept back any thing from me but thee, because thou art his wife: how then can I do this great wickedness, and sin against God?" Genesis 39: 9.

Clearly, Joseph knew, or at least assumed, that having sex with someone who he was not married to violated the will of his God. Remember, this was a time well before God gave the Ten Commandments to the nation of Israel, so Joseph was not simply dutifully heeding the "thou shall not commit adultery" commandment- he had never heard of it. The laws and desires of God in this area had been communicated to him in some other manner. The story is a great illustration of my conclusions in this book elsewhere that obeying the laws of God are a form of joy, and also a form of joyful worship of Him. All of us should experience joy in our lives when we follow the will of God and obey his commandments in the face of severe temptation to indulge in greatly pleasurable, but sinful behaviors.

Ray Eichenberger

SEXY SONG OF SOLOMON

My postulate herein that sex must have something to do with the joy and exultation of our worship of God was developed when considering several different factors. First, the references to sex and the sexual antics of the inhabitants of the Old Testament often seem quite superfluous and unnecessary. We have already stated that the narratives of the weird sexual liaisons of Abraham with both Sarah and Hagar might be explained by a desire to give the history of the ethnic and clan divisions in the history of Israel and the Middle East. Similarly, the illustrations of the bad sexual behaviors of Abraham, Jacob, King David, and King Solomon could also be explained as providing very much negative examples of the mayhem and generally messiness which are soon to follow when we violate God's chosen plan for our sex lives, marriages, and family. A more tongue-in-

THE GOD ORGASM

cheek reason as to why there is so much sex and so many sexual references in the Bible might well be that the God-inspired writers and scriveners of Scripture might simply have included those stories to make the Word of God more entertaining and appealing to certain people. But, the most vivid examples of sex in the pages of the Bible, almost seeming to be overtly sensually erotic in nature, are found in the Song of Solomon in the Old Testament.

I was in junior high school, sitting in a Sunday school class, when I was first introduced to the great erotic poetry of the Bible. No, it was not being taught by the approved teacher in our Lutheran Sunday school curriculum. During the midst of a lesson about Moses or Noah or someone else in the Old Testament for the tenth or twentieth time in my Sunday-school-since-a-toddler career, a male classmate passed a note to check out the steamy passages of the Song of Solomon. The male inhabitants of the class immediately turned to that Old Testament Book, and a distracting din soon hit the classroom as we all started a mostly juvenile giggle about the passages that we were reading.

Ray Eichenberger

The poor Sunday school teacher walked over to see what we were doing, knowingly smiled, shook his head, and asked us to return to the study of Moses or Abraham or whomever. He politely suggested that we could explore the sexual side of the Bible on our own time, and not on his classroom time. This man was one of my favorite and most memorable Sunday school teachers, and I'm certain that he went home and shared the story with his wife, and that they got a good laugh about the typical behavior of adolescent boys, even in a church Sunday School environment. It would have been hard to compete with poetry containing sexual content when teaching my age group at the time.

Regardless of my first experience with the Song of Solomon, it remains a very erotic and beautiful section of our Bible.

The story narrated by the Song of Solomon is quite simply explained. And, yes, the book's prose was supposedly written by King Solomon himself, although the authorship has been hotly debated by Bible scholars from time to time. Ancient authorities on the Bible accepted it as being written by the King of the same name. The book tells the story of a girl who was taken from her home in the region of Shunem by King Solomon. The girl was beautiful and stunning, and she had the misfortune to be seen by the King alongside the roadway. Once again, she was snatched away by the King to be used sexually by him. The Shunamite woman was a shepherd, and she was madly in love with a fellow male shepherd when she was kidnapped and taken away by Solomon to Jerusalem.

Therefore, the Shunamite woman of the Song of Solomon had been wrenched away from her native home, her family members, and the man who she was totally in love with. Her destiny was to become a concubine or wife to King Solomon, who we have already learned had too many wives and too many concubines- far more than he would have ever known what to do with and to keep occupied.

The verses of the Song of Solomon immediately delve into the pining of and the desires of the Shunamite woman for the man that she loved. The man is unnamed, and a knowledge of the story and background of the lady make it clear that she is certainly not infatuated with her captor and master, the King, in her language and poetry. Immediately, the longings of the woman for her lost lover are comparable to the great romantic literature and the great romantic metaphors of the ages. "Let him kiss me with the kisses of his mouth; for thy love is better than wine. Because of the savour of thy good ointments thy name is as ointment poured forth, therefore do the virgins love thee. Draw me, we will run after thee, the king hath brought me into his chambers; we will be glad and rejoice in thee, we will remember thy love more than wine: the upright love thee." Song of Solomon 1: 2-4.

The images of the above verses are very intense. King Solomon may well have taken the young, lovely woman to his bed, to indulge in his royal prerogatives with her, but her thoughts and desires were not for the wealthiest, wisest man in the world, but for her true love and fellow shepherd.

The only other intensely personal, descriptive portion of the story is found in the following verse, where the woman states, "I am black, but comely, O ye daughters of Jerusalem, as the tents of Kedar, as the curtains of Solomon." Song of Solomon 1: 5. As a result, we can assume that the Shunamite woman was a black skinned woman, possibly from a region of Africa when she was snatched up and taken away by Solomon.

THE GOD ORGASM

The erotic beauty and poetry of the Song of Solomon is very much evidenced by the writing skills of the author, as the words melodically relate the descriptions of the Shunamite woman's true lover. "I have compared thee, O my love, to a company of horses in Pharaoh's chariots. Thy cheeks are comely with rows of jewels, thy neck with chains of gold. We will make thee borders of gold with studs of silver. While the king sitteth at his table, my spikenard sendeth forth the smell thereof. A bundle of myrrh is my well beloved unto me: he shall lie all night between my breasts. My beloved is unto me as a cluster of camphire in the vineyard of Engedi. Behold, thou art fair, my love; behold, thou art fair; thou hast doves' eyes. Behold, thou art fair, my beloved, yea, pleasant; also our bed is green. The beams of our houses are cedar and our rafters of fir." Song of Solomon 1: 9-17.

The Shunamite woman also uses her great poetic and earthy skills to describe herself as she pines away for her true love, the shepherd, who is lost to her. "I am the rose of Sharon, and the lily of the valleys. As the lily among thorns, so is my love among the daughters. As the apple tree among the trees of the wood, so is my beloved among the sons. I sat down under his shadow with great delight, and his fruit was sweet to my taste. He brought me to the banqueting house, and his banner over me was love. Stay me with flagons, comfort me with apples; for I am sick of love. His left hand is under my head, and his right hand doth embrace me. I charge you, O ye daughters of Jerusalem, by the roes, and by the hinds of the field, that ye stir not up, nor awake my love, till he please." Song of Solomon 2: 1-7.

The Shunamite woman's descriptions of her lover then becomes very sexual, and sensual, and still serves to convey the great love between the couple, as opposed to merely erotic lust. "The voice of my beloved! Behold, he cometh leaping upon the mountains, skipping upon the hills. My beloved is like a roe or a young hart: behold, he standeth behind our wall, he looketh forth at the windows, shewing himself through the lattice. My beloved spake, and said unto me, Rise up, my love, my fair one and come away. For, lo, the winter is past and the rain is over and gone; The flowers appear on the earth, the time of the singing of birds is come, and the voice of the turtle is heard in our land; The fig tree putteth forth her green figs, and the vines with the tender grape give a good smell. Arise, my love, my fair one, and come away. O my dove, that art in the clefts of the rock, in the secret places of the stairs, let me see thy countenance, let me hear thy voice: for sweet is thy voice, and thy countenance is comely. Take us the foxes, the little foxes, that spoil the vines: for our vines have tender grapes. My beloved is mine, and I am his: he feedeth among the lilies. Until the day break, and the shadows flee away, turn my beloved, and be thou like a roe or a young hart upon the mountains of Bether." Song of Solomon 2: 8-17.

I can see in the preceding passages a desire by our lady to see her lover, and a bittersweet homesickness for her lost love and her family. It is fun to speculate that perhaps the lover of the Shunamite woman was able to travel to Jerusalem, and to gain fleeting glimpses of his lady fair, or perhaps even to sneak stolen encounters and meetings with the woman. The text of the Song of Solomon certainly hints of those factors in our story.

The love struck and forlorn Shunamite woman then searched for her lost lover- "By night on my bed I sought him whom my soul loveth: I sought him, but I found him not. I will rise now, and go about the city in the streets, and in the broad ways I will seek him whom my soul loveth: I sought him, but I found him not. The watchman that go about the city found me: to whom I said, Saw ye him whom my soul loveth? It was but a little that I passed from them, but I found him who my soul loveth; I held him, and would not let him go, until I had brought him into my mother's house, and into the chamber of her that conceived me." Song of Solomon 3: 1-4.

Chapter 4 of the Song of Solomon poetically and metaphorically rises up and creates further very erotic descriptions of the Shunamite woman, this time from the perspective of her fellow and lost love, the shepherd. The prose is worthy of any great love story, or of a modern-day soliloquy between forlorn lovers. "Behold, thou art fair, my love; behold, thou art fair; thou hast dove's eyes within thy locks: thy hair is as a flock of goats, that appear from Mount Gilead. Thy teeth are like a flock of sheep that are even shorn, which came up from the washing: whereof every one bear twins, and none is barren among them. Thy lips are like a thread of scarlet, and thy speech is comely; thy temples are like a piece of a pomegranate within thy locks. Thy neck is like the tower of David builded for an armoury, whereon there hang a thousand bucklers, all shields of mighty men. Thy two breasts are like two young roes that are twins, which feed among the lilies. Until the day break and the shadows flee away, I will get me to the mountain of myrrh, and to the hill of frankincense. Thou art all fair, my love, there is no spot in thee." Song of Solomon 4: 1-7. The erotic metaphors concerning "the mountain of myrrh" and the "hill of frankincense" should be very apparent to modern man. My imagination was very active when I read those lines and considered the author's prose.

Other metaphors and comparisons in the above passage may not sound very alluring in modern language ("thy teeth are like a flock of sheep," and other allusions to the flock), but the descriptions would undoubtedly be very meaningful to the Shunamite shepherds who spent their hours with each other and with the herds of their four-legged charges.

The descriptions of the Shunamite damsel by her male lover continue very passionately, "How fair is thy love, my sister, my spouse! how much better is thy love than wine! and the smell of thine ointments than all spices! Thy lips, O my spouse, drop as the honeycomb: honey and milk are under thy tongue; and the smell of thy garments is like the smell of Lebanon. A garden inclosed is my sister, my spouse; a spring shut up, a fountain sealed. They plants are an orchard of pomegranates, with pleasant fruits; camphire, with spikenard. Spikenard and saffron: calamus and cinnamon, with all trees of frankincense; myrrh and aloes, with all the chief spices; A fountain of gardens, a well of living waters, and streams from Lebanon. Awake, O north wind and come, thou south: blow upon my garden, that the spices thereof may flow out. Let my beloved come into his garden, and eat his pleasant fruits." Song of Solomon 4: 10-16. I don't have a difficult time imagining the smells and tastes of fruit as being erotic in nature. Certain other odors, such as the smell of warm cinnamon mentioned in the verses, are some of the more pleasurable fragrances on earth and my personal favorites.

In Chapter 5 the Shunamite woman experiences the joy of an anticipated meeting with her lover, but she also encounters the after-pains of sorrow when the man and woman do not link up with each other. "I rose up to open to my beloved; and my hands dropped with myrrh, and my fingers with sweet

THE GOD ORGASM

smelling myrrh, upon the handles of the lock. I opened to my beloved, but my beloved had withdrawn himself, and was gone; my soul failed when he spake: I sought him, but I could not find him; I called him, but he gave me no answer. The watchmen that went about the city found me, they smote me, they wounded me; the keepers of the walls took away my vail from me. I charge you, O daughters of Jerusalem, if ye find my beloved, that ye tell him, that I am sick of love." Song of Solomon 5: 5-8.

What a powerful passage! The Shulamite woman exalted when she thought that she would see and meet with her lover, but she experienced great pain when she was away from him. "I am sick of love" is both poignant and a truism. Most human beings have experienced the same feelings of the sometimes lonely and frustrating nature of being in love. But, this slave of Solomon was also subjected to physical pain because of her situation, along with the emotional pain. Solomon's guards in the city found her out wandering, searching for her lover at night, and the Shunamite woman declares that she was physically beaten by those cruel men of the army.

The "sick of love" feeling was both fickle and fleeting, though, as in the same Chapter she again muses on the physical attributes of her lover. "What is thy beloved more than another beloved, O thou fairest among women? what is thy beloved more than another beloved, that thou dost so charge us? My beloved is white and ruddy, the chiefest among the ten thousand. His head is as the most fine gold, his locks are bushy, and black as a raven. His eyes are as the eyes of doves, by the rivers of waters, washed with milk, and fitly set. His cheeks are as a bed of spices, as sweet flowers: his lips like lilies, dropping sweet smelling myrrh. His hands are as gold rings set with the beryl: his belly is as bright ivory overlaid with sapphires. His legs are as pillars of marble, set upon sockets of fine gold: his countenance is as Lebanon, excellent as the cedars. His mouth is most sweet; yea, he is altogether lovely. This is my beloved, and this is my friend, O daughters of Jerusalem." Song of Solomon 5: 9-16.

The erotica between our Shunamite couple continues in Chapter 6, with further very vivid images of the human body and physical love. "Whither is thy beloved gone, O thou fairest among women? whither is they beloved turned aside?

THE GOD ORGASM

That we may seek him with thee. My beloved is gone down into his garden, to the beds of spices, to feed in the gardens, and to gather lilies. I am my beloved's and my beloved is mine; he feedeth among the lilies." Song of Solomon 6: 1-3.

In a humorous passage, and in a very stark editorial comment about her plight, the Shunamite woman (very dangerously I would imagine) has some very choice words about the excesses and greed of King Solomon in taking her away from her lover and her family. "There are threescore queens, and fourscore concubines, and virgins without number. My dove, my undefiled, is but one, she is the only one of her mother." Song of Solomon 6: 8-9.

The vivid descriptions of the physical attributes of the Shunamite woman continue in Chapter 7. "How beautiful are thy feet with shoes, O prince's daughter! The joints of thy thighs are like jewels, the work of the hands of a cunning workman. Thy navel is like a round goblet, which wanteth not liquor: they belly is like a heap of wheat set about with lilies. Thy two breasts are like two young roes that are twins. Thy neck is a tower of ivory; thine eyes like the fishpools in Heshbon, by the gate of Bathrabbim: thy nose is as the tower of Lebanon which looketh toward Damascus. Thine head upon thee is like Carmel, and the hair of thine head like purple; the king is held in the galleries. How fair and how pleasant art thou, O love, for delights. This thy stature is like to a palm tree, and thy breasts to clusters of grapes. I said, I will go up to the palm tree, I will take hold of the boughs thereof, now also thy breasts shall be as clusters of the vine, and the smell of they nose like apples: And the roof of thy mouth like the best wine for my beloved, that goeth down sweetly, causing the lips of those that are asleep to speak." Song of Solomon 7: 1-9.

Interestingly again, the latter part of Chapter 7 refers to several different types of plants and fruits. "Let us get up early to the vineyards; let us see if the vine flourish, whether the tender grape appear, and the pomegranates bud forth: there will I give thee my loves. The mandrakes give a smell, and at our gates are all manner of pleasant fruits, new and old, which I have laid up for thee, O my beloved." Song of Solomon 7: 12-13. This is at least the second passage in the Bible which mentions the powerful sexual stimulus of mandrakes, or love apples. Recall that the first famous passages about that fruit occurred in the book of Genesis, where the warring sister-wives of Jacob, Leah and Rachel, contended over the mandrakes found by Leah's son, Reuben. Leah had been bearing children for Jacob, and Rachel had not been able to conceive for Jacob again. In those passages, Rachel agreed to send Jacob into Leah for a night of the sexual favors of her husband, if Rachel would then be given the power of Reuben's aphrodisiac-like mandrakes to use. See, Genesis 30: 9-24. Leah conceived a child for Jacob after bargaining for the mandrakes, and Rachel must have also made good use of the stimulant plant, for she too became pregnant and bore Joseph soon after this event. Genesis 30: 22-24.

Song of Solomon concludes in Chapter 8 with a reaffirmation of our lovers' devotion to each other, with more arousing descriptive and language. "O that thou wert as my brother, that sucked the breasts of my mother! When I should find thee without, I would kiss thee: yea, I should not be despised. I would lead thee, and bring thee into my mother's house, who would instruct me: I would cause thee to drink of spiced wine of the juice of my pomegranate. His left hand should be under my head, and his right hand should embrace me. I charge you, O daughters of Jerusalem, that ye stir not up, nor awake my love, until he please. Who is that that cometh up from the wilderness, leaning upon her beloved? I raised thee up under the apple tree; there thy mother brought thee forth: thence she brought thee forth that bare thee. Set me as a seal upon thy heart, as a seal upon thine arm: for love is strong as death; jealousy is cruel as the grave: the coals thereof are coals of fire, which hath a most vehement flame. Many waters cannot quench love, neither can the floods drown it: if a man would give all the substance of his house for love, it would utterly be condemned. We have a little sister, and she hath no breasts: what shall we do for our sister in the day when she shall be spoken for? If she be a wall, we will build upon her a palace of silver; and if she be a door, we will inclose her with boards of cedar. I am a wall, and my breasts like towers; then was I in his eyes as one that found favour." Song of Solomon 8: 1-10. This passage is filled with many, many beautiful and descriptive words. "Love is strong as death," and "many waters cannot quench love" are included in these powerful passages, and are worthy as the finest phrases about the power of love ever written.

THE GOD ORGASM

The mighty ode to love and physical beauty concludes with the erotic statement, "Make hast, my beloved, and be thou like to a roe or to a young hart upon the mountains of spices." Song of Solomon 8: 14.

I could read the Song of Solomon over and over again, for its beautiful descriptive language is vivid, alluring and seductive.

As the Song of Solomon concludes, we can ask ourselves, again, why are these very erotic passages and stories included in the pages of the Old Testament? Very many Bible commentators have described the language of the Song as a prophetic foretelling of the love and passion of Jesus Christ for His church and for His Saints. I can also see such imagery in the prose of the Song of Solomon, and it becomes even more meaningful and useful with that in mind.

In other words, is the erotic language of the Song of Solomon an allegory for the love which God wants to extend to us in our relationship with Him? Is the inclusion of the Song of Solomon in the Old Testament a kind of guide as to how sensual and joyful and loving God wants our relationship with Him and the Lord Jesus Christ to be? Is the prose of the

Ray Eichenberger

Song of Solomon a revelation as to what our future eternity in Heaven spent with our God will look like? I would have thought that it was just an interesting personal theory, and perhaps an unsubstantiated personal revelation of sorts, until I remembered and turned to the back pages of the New Testament. Will at least a part of the joy of Heaven for us include the joy of worshipping God through what the finite mind of man can only now describe as sensual or sexual-like experiences?

THE GOD ORGASM

ETERNAL JOY OF SEX?

Think of the most sensual experiences that you have ever encountered during your existence and time living on our Earth. The experiences might be sexual- some of mine are. It might bring to mind a time that you were stunned and awed by the beauty of nature and a panoramic view that struck your senses to such an extent that you will never forget it- for me, the Grand Canyon, Death Valley, Yosemite National Park, the slot canyons near Lake Powell, Arizona, Yellowstone National Park, Grand Teton National Park, and the vistas on several islands of Hawaii were such experiences. Just staring at the ocean while on a boat, from the perspective of being in the middle of it, and seeing nothing but beautiful, blue water surrounding you also does that for me. The sensory and visual pleasures of life as conveyed through nature and God's creations are capable of giving us goose-bumps and stimulating our senses. These sensory experiences should lend themselves to joyfully worshipping our God.

Then, if you are a parent, think of the awe and wonder you felt and experienced when you witnessed the birth of your child or children. The beginning of life, the reality that you created a new person, and that the person you created is a gift from our God, all combined to create an intense mental and spiritual high and euphoria.

Turn your mind's eye to that sensual feeling, that feeling of awe and wonder. Listen to your mind and try to recall how you physically and mentally felt at the experiences of sensuality that came to you in these memories, both physical and mental. That, my friend, should be the sensual experience and feeling that we receive and encounter each time that we begin to worship God- whether it be a church service, reading his Word, listening to Christian music, or spending deep and meaningful time conversing with God in our prayer lives.

The sexual content of the Old Testament and the Song of Solomon might well just be sub-themes of the Bible, and my stated tongue-in-cheek desire to spice up the reading and to

THE GOD ORGASM

keep people interested in the Book in general, were it not for the sexual imagery which then appears in one of the most important statements of the Bible- the Book of Revelation. And, as we shall study herein, the Book of Revelation time and time again describes our final relationship with God and Jesus Christ in Heaven and at the end times using similar sexual imagery and metaphors, such as are found in the Song of Solomon.

What struck me as very interesting initially on this topic, at the start of Revelation, was the fact that God describes the evil actors of the earth, and their actions, in very negative sexual terms. In the middle of the praises, and warnings to the various churches at the start of Revelation, John revealed messages to the church at Thyatira. That church first received compliments for some of their works, charity, patience, and service, but then was rocked with a dire and ominous warning. "Notwithstanding I have a few things against thee, because thou sufferest that woman Jezebel, which calleth herself a prophetess, to teach and to seduce my servants to commit fornication, and to eat things sacrificed unto idols. And I gave her space to repent of her fornication; and she repented not.

Behold, I will cast her into a bed, and them that commit adultery with her into great tribulation, except they repent of their deeds. And I will kill her children with death; and all the churches shall know that I am he which searcheth the reins and hearts: and I will give unto every one of you according to your works." Revelation 2: 20-23. Teaching and seducing the saints to violate the Word and Laws of God are described as fornication. Then, the punishment for such behavior is described as thrown into a bed, and experiencing the great tribulation there, presumably in my mind by having a lifetime of debased and meaningless sex. In other parts of the Bible, such Godless actions are threatened with the result of being cast into the fires of hell, with the accompanying torments and suffering. But, in Revelation 2, the behaviors are described as deserving of the inability to communicate with God on a deep, passionate, spiritual level, such as the sensual joys of experiencing a complete union with Him.

Similarly, as the story of Revelation nears the end of the book with narratives of the final judgments upon enemies, the Great Tribulation, and the New Jerusalem, God through John once again employs negative sexual metaphors and

THE GOD ORGASM

descriptions to describe the workings of the evil enemies of God. "And there came one of the seven angels which had the seven vials, and talked with me, saying unto me, Come hither; I will shew unto thee the judgment of the great whore that sitteth upon many waters: With whom the kings of the earth have committed fornication, and the inhabitants of the earth have been made drunk with the wine of her fornication. So he carried me away in the spirit into the wilderness: and I saw a woman sit upon a scarlet coloured beast, full of names of blasphemy, having seven heads and ten horns. And the woman was arrayed in purple and scarlet colour, and decked with gold and precious stones and pearls, having a golden cup in her hand full of abominations and filthiness of her fornication: And upon her forehead was a name written, MYSTERY, BABYLON THE GREAT, THE MOTHER OF HARLOTS AND ABOMINATIONS OF THE EARTH. And I saw the woman drunken with the blood of the saints, and with the blood of the martyrs of Jesus: and when I saw her, I wondered with great admiration. And the angel said unto me, Wherefore didst thou marvel? I will tell thee the mystery of the woman, and of the beast that carrieth her, which hath the seven heads and ten horns." Revelation 17: 1-7.

The evil and powerful woman who was capable of seducing Kings of the earth is described as a harlot, a woman who abuses the God-given joy and euphoria of sex with Godless and amoral lovers, and who is paid for her services. The fact that the description of the harlot is an allegory is later explained towards the end of Revelation 17. "And he saith unto me, The waters which thou sawest, where the whore sitteth, are peoples, and multitudes, and nations, and tongues. And the ten horns which thou sawest upon the beast, these shall hate the whore, and shall make her desolate and naked, and shall eat her flesh, and burn her with fire. For God hath put in their hearts to fulfil his will, and to agree, and give their kingdom unto the beast, until the words of God shall be fulfilled. And the woman which thou sawest is that great city, which reigneth over the kings of the earth." Revelation 17: 15-18. The metaphor and allegorical nature of the language is certainly not complicated, and can easily be discerned, but, once again, why use the language at all, and why pose the evil actress as a character who is sexually perverted? Why isn't the

THE GOD ORGASM

language of Revelation 17 simply stated by describing the decadence of Babylon by name, rather than being like an evil, sexually promiscuous woman who has fought against God and His laws?

As if that example and language in Revelation 17 is not sufficient, much the same themes and descriptions are repeated in Revelation 18 which follows. "And after these things I saw another angel come down from heaven, having great power; and the earth was lightened with his glory. And he cried mightily with a strong voice, saying, Babylon the great is fallen, is fallen, and is become the habitation of devils, and the hold of every foul spirit, and a cage of every unclean and hateful bird. For all nations have drunk of the wine of the wrath of her fornication, and the kings of the earth have committed fornication with her, and the merchants of the earth are waxed rich through the abundance of her delicacies. And I heard another voice from heaven, saying, Come out of her, my people, that ye be not partakers of her sins, and that ye receive not of her plagues. For her sins have reached unto heaven, and God hath remembered her iniquities. Reward her even as she rewarded you, and double unto her double according to her works: in the cup which she hath filled fill to her double. How much she hath glorified herself, and lived deliciously, so much torment and sorrow give her: for she saith in her heart, I sit a queen, and am no widow, and shall see no sorrow. Therefore shall her plagues come in one day, death, and mourning, and famine; and she shall be utterly burned with fire: for strong is the Lord God who judgeth her. And the kings of the earth, who have committed fornication and lived deliciously with her, shall bewail her, and lament for her, when they shall see the smoke of her burning, Standing afar off for the fear of her torment, saying, Alas, alas that great city Babylon, that mighty city! for in one hour is thy judgment come." Revelation 18: 1-10.

The evil actions of Jezebel, the harlot, the Kings, and other powers of the earth in fornicating with the followers of Satan are then directly contrasted in the subsequent chapters of Revelation. And, it is these final chapters where I find the language that makes me believe and realize that God wants our worship of Him to be so intense, so exhilarating, and so joyful, as to be similar to and like the joy and sensuality humans encounter in the sexual nature of our lives. The first

THE GOD ORGASM

and very clear statement of this is found in Revelation 18, where God bluntly states in the hearing of John, "Let us be glad and rejoice, and give honour to him, for the marriage of the lamb is come, and his wife hath made herself ready." Revelation 18: 7. It is very obvious in other parts of Scripture and Revelation that the bride of Jesus is to be the Church, including all of us as His Followers. "And I, John, saw the holy city, new Jerusalem, coming down from God out of heaven, prepared as a bride adorned for her husband." Revelation 21: 2.

This theme is continued in the following verses in Revelation 21. "And there came unto me one of the seven angels which had the seven vials full of the seven last plagues, and talked with me, saying, Come hither, I will shew thee the bride, the Lamb's wife. And he carried me away in the spirit to a great and high mountain, and shewed me that great city, the holy Jerusalem, descending out of heaven from God." Revelation 21: 9-10.

The key verses of Revelation as to the euphoria and joy and awesome wonder of Heaven being compared to the sensual pleasures of having sex then occur. "Let us be glad and

165

rejoice, and give honour to him: for the marriage of the Lamb is come, and his wife hath made herself ready. And to her was granted that she should be arrayed in fine linen, clean and white: for the fine linen is the righteousness of saints. And he saith unto me, Write, Blessed are they which are called unto the marriage supper of the Lamb. And he saith unto me, These are the true sayings of God." Revelation 19: 7-9.

A brief digression is necessary here to provide information necessary for the culmination of this chapter. The Israeli engagement and wedding customs in the time of Jesus had several distinctive stages. First, the initial ketubah rite involved what in modern times we would call the engagement of the couple. The matching of a male and female were predominantly created by families, and it might be very loose to call the female a woman in our modern sense. Very often, young teenage girls were betrothed to be married in a ketubah, perhaps even children. For example, it is often speculated that when the Gospels say that Mary and Joseph were betrothed before the conception of Jesus during their ketubah, that Mary may have been as young as twelve to fourteen years old. See

THE GOD ORGASM

Matthew 1: 18-25, as to this initial ketubah betrothal of the Holy Couple.

Then, chronologically, the lag time between the ketubah and the actual consummation of the marriage, the wedding feast, and living together as a family unit as husband and wife may have been very long. Most scholars believe that the sexual consummation of the engaged couple occurred before the wedding feast, with the close relatives of both the bride and groom waiting outside of the "bedroom" for proof of the bloody sheets and bedding which signaled the evidence of a virgin bride having performed her first act of intimacy with her man. The description of that scene, if at all true, strikes me as a very public and far less than intimate conclusion of what instead should be a very intimate and alluring time. If you attempt to translate that scenario to our modern times and customs, the imagery becomes quite bizarre.

The joyful celebration of the wedding feast did not occur until everyone was satisfied that the bride was indeed a virgin being presented to her husband.

As a result of the above cultural traditions and mores concerning Jewish marriage in the time of Jesus, consider what Revelation is saying about the role of the church as the bride of Jesus, fully prepared to engage and take an active part in the wedding feast of the Lamb.

The bride of Christ metaphor is surreal and awesome. The visual picture of a wholesome bride on her wedding night presenting herself untouched and perfect (for all of us in Heaven, now perfect) to her groom is compelling. Both parties to this union shed their clothes and present themselves, undefiled to the other party. The bodies become one in an intense emotional and physical union, and each of their senses are magnified and stirred because of this encounter. The emotions and sensations build and explode into an awesome climax of body and soul uniting together and satisfying each other.

Is it possible (and I certainly believe that it is), that a large part of our time in Heaven and our communion with our Gods (the Trinity, of course), involves God, the Lord Jesus Christ, and the Holy Spirit entering into our perfected bodies? It is possible that the members of the Trinity join together with us by fully enveloping our hearts, souls, and minds, and creating for us what we only have the limited capabilities to describe as a sensual, euphoric, and orgasmic union with our God? The thought of that makes me shudder as I write these words, and the thought of a periodic, perfect union with my God and the sensations and sensualities involved in doing so totally boggles my very finite and way too limited mind.

And, no, I'm not suggesting that God and the other members of the Trinity unite with all of us as Saints in Heaven in what we understand to be the physical and crude nature of the physical sex act here on Earth. I have no idea of the logistics of the marriage supper of the Lamb, and if my God would wish to have, in my very limited and finite understanding, what would be a physical act of sex with me. If that indeed is what occurs in Heaven, bring it on. The metaphor of the potter and the clay again comes to mind in the fact that God can do to me as his servant whatever he wishes to do. Isaiah 64: 8. Romans 9: 19-24.

And, I'm certainly not suggesting that all of us as Christians form some sort of weird cult where we have Sunday morning church services which consist of having sex with our brother and sister congregants, so as to reach the euphoria of using sex to trigger the joy and awe of experiencing and worshipping God (but, see the concluding chapter to follow).

In the words of the Book of Revelation, particularly Revelation 21 which we have discussed in this Chapter, I find hope in the ultimate, joyful, sensual, and overwhelming experiences to come in Heaven as we all combine to worship our God. The joy of worship should be similar to the joy of experiencing sexual euphoria- satisfaction, overwhelming sensual feelings and senses, and an intensity that we encounter nowhere else in our lives as human beings.

Although I have no Biblical support for my personal beliefs and hopes expressed above (except the language of Revelation cited herein), imagine this ultimate experience. You are in Heaven. On a regular basis, a member of the Trinity visits you and somehow enters your body. You have the opportunity and privilege to completely and fully join with the God of Heaven as you become one with His soul, even for a brief moment. What an awesome opportunity to truly worship and to perfectly unite with our God.

As I leave my theories and hopes for an intimate relationship with our God in Heaven, the actual promises of

THE GOD ORGASM

Revelation as to our afterlife with God are chilling and awesome enough, even if my longings do not turn out to be correct at all. "And I heard a great voice out of heaven saying, Behold, the tabernacle of God is with men, and he will dwell with them, and they shall be his people, and God himself shall be with them, and be their God. And God shall wipe away all tears from their eyes; and there shall be no more death, neither sorrow, nor crying, neither shall there be any more pain: for the former things are passed away." Revelation 21: 3-4. "And he shewed me a pure river of water of life, clear as crystal, proceeding out of the throne of God and of the Lamb. In the midst of the street of it, and on either side of the river, was there the tree of life, which bare twelve manner of fruits, and yielded her fruit every month: and the leaves of the tree were for the healing of the nations. And there shall be no more curse: but the throne of God and of the Lamb shall be in it; and his servants shall serve him: And they shall see his face; and his name shall be in their foreheads. And there shall be no night there; and they need no candle, neither light of the sun; for the Lord God giveth them light: and they shall reign for ever and ever." Revelation 22: 1-5

Ray Eichenberger

Amen and amen, as we all wait for the fulfillment of those promises and the joyful exhilaration of spending our eternities in Heaven with our Lord and Maker.

THE GOD ORGASM

DAILY JOY IN GOD

As we wait for the joys of worshipping our God in Heaven, how then can we increase the joy of our worship here on Earth, and in our personal Christian walks? It immediately strikes me that our joy about God, positively or negatively, is very obvious to those around us, particularly to those who don't yet know Jesus Christ. Those people see us and view us as the only available examples as to how Godly people act, even if we don't consciously think of that fact all of the time. Perhaps not consciously thinking about that very topic all of the time is the crux of the problem. In other words, a sour and joyless Christian comes across to others and non-believers as a person who knows God, but is not any different than the rest of the inhabitants of this planet as to their lack of concern, lack of compassion, and lack of an upbeat and optimistic attitude as to how they approach life and other people.

I find the key to leading a joyful life and worshipping God in that manner is being able to overcome the cares and concerns of life while still being able to approach and worship God with the exhilaration that we have already discussed. In other words, your joy in God and Jesus Christ are not dependent on your temporary life situations and problems and woes which you encounter at any given time in our existences.

Scriptures are full of admonitions to rise above our circumstances in retaining a joyful relationship with God, in spite of our own personal needs, wants, and trials. The book of James famously states, "My brethren, count it all joy when ye fall into divers temptations." James 1: 2. Likewise, the Apostle Paul taught, "In every thing give thanks: for this is the will of God in Christ Jesus concerning you." I Thessalonians 5: 18.

I did not want to end this work about re-creating our worship of God to increase our joy in Him without first giving some very practical examples about how to do just that.

THE GOD ORGASM

PHYSICALLY WORSHIP GOD

Too often it seems that all of us just treat the joyful worship of our God as a mental exercise. We're listening to a Scripture reading in church, or we're trying to listen to and digest the pastor's sermon every week. And, there may not be a whole lot of joy which comes to your mind when you only mentally participate in those things.

But, conversely, joyful worship should be an action verb and phrase- the art of doing and physically immersing yourself in the activity of praising and worshipping our God and the Lord Jesus Christ. In any event, it is always much more stimulating and fun for me in any day to day activity if I'm active and physically involved in the task I am performing. The action and the movement of the body seems to focus-in my ever-wandering concentration as well.

I am a huge movie fan, and I have already joked previously in this work that several of my favorite cinematic scenes of praise and worship are in unlikely movies. First, I recall the black gospel church scene in the film Forrest Gump, after Forrest builds a new church for the late Bubba's congregation with his newly acquired wealth from being a "shrimp boat captain." The film shows a gospel choir singing an enthusiastic spiritual or gospel song, and the entire congregation seems to be swaying and gyrating- the place is rocking. Lieutenant Dan is even in the back of the church sanctuary, sitting in his wheelchair and listening to the worship.

I have already mentioned herein that by far my favorite movie scene of worship probably borders on the bizarre. Jake and Elwood Blues, in the Blues Brothers film, visit a congregation led by the reverend James Brown. Once again, the gospel music during the service is pulsating and lively, and the entire congregation is physically involved in the beat by swaying and raucous worship. Congregation members are doing somersaults and cartwheels in the aisles. James Brown intones something about "seeing the light" and the Blues Brothers join the rowdy worship celebration by dancing and performing gymnastics. While my description seems even more bizarre when putting it to writing, the worship celebration just seems downright fun. And, I also firmly assert that God would believe that it is a righteous form of joyful and enjoyable worship of Him as well.

THE GOD ORGASM

Since we're not all going to dance in the aisles of our local church and perform somersaults and cartwheels, we can physically do several other things as we worship our God. First, I often find myself swaying and almost dancing to the beat of a lively worship song on a Sunday morning. I have a background from my public school student days of playing a band instrument and singing in both school and church choirs. I love all sorts and kinds of music, so it doesn't take much for me to enjoy and react to the melodies and beats of any song.

The most common form of physical worship in modern America seems to be raising hands and arms to Heaven as we worship our God. As I mentioned at the start of this work, I come from a Lutheran church background as a youth, which was solidly conservative and which provided a very underwhelming quiet and reserved atmosphere for worship. I can vividly remember a time when I was a teen in our Lutheran Sunday morning service when a visitor to the service began crying out "Amens," and "Hallelujahs" during the sermon of our then elderly pastor. While the overly frumpy numbers of the congregation did not actually laugh at the vocally robust worshipper, it was very easy to tell that most people were not comfortable with the joyful verbal responses to the message that morning. You could almost feel a wave of tuts and clucks overwhelm the atmosphere of our sanctuary.

The lifting up of hands and arms was also never performed in our staid, conservative Lutheran church of my youth. As a result, when I started attending churches as an adult where people actually lifted up their hands and arms to God, I found it unfamiliar and peculiar, and felt more than a little awkward doing it. But, the active nature of physical worship by lifting hands and arms finally grew on me. And, I discovered that it seemed like a natural, intimate way to express my joy in worship by doing that, when I was moved by the Spirit to express myself in that manner.

The physical act of worshipping in that manner is deeply embedded in our Bible, and mentioned repeatedly in various passages. "Thus will I bless thee while I live: I will lift up my hands in thy name." Psalm 63: 4. "I will therefore that men pray every where, lifting up holy hands, without wrath and doubting." I Timothy 2: 8. "Lift up your hands in the sanctuary, and bless the Lord." Psalms 134: 2. "Let my prayer be set forth before thee as incense; and the lifting up of my hands as the evening sacrifice." Psalm 141:2.

One of the mightiest kings depicted in the Bible, and the wealthiest, King Solomon, humbled himself before God in his worship and used this physical action to praise his God. "And it was so, that when Solomon had made an end of praying all this prayer and supplication unto the Lord, he arose from before the altar of the Lord, from kneeling on his knees with his hands spread up to heaven." I Kings 8: 54.

The physical act of kneeling before the Lord is also mentioned several times in the Old Testament, as a joyful and reverent method to praise and glorify God. The Book of Nehemiah adds another nuance to praying and praising God on one's knees. "And Ezra blessed the Lord, the great God. And all the people answered, Amen, Amen, with lifting up their hands: and they bowed their heads, and worshipped the Lord with their faces to the ground." Nehemiah 8: 6. Alas, I am growing older, and will probably not be bowing my forehead to the ground in my worship on a Sunday morning- the mind and spirit are willing, but I would not be getting back up to my feet very readily and without a great deal of assistance. But, prostrating your whole body before God in prayer and praise does strike me as a joyful and reverent way to worship on a Sunday morning in church, or during any daily time of worship to our God.

I have observed people using their hands and arms to worship God in several different ways. Most people in the church I attend simply stretch their hands and arms above their heads and appear that they are reaching out to attempt to grab onto our God. After all, that is precisely what that physical gesture should mean. We are reaching for God's blessings, and acknowledging the power, might, and creative ability of our God. The image of our hands raised to Heaven and to God is also one of need and expectation- the raised hands are inviting God to provide for us and to sustain us both physically and spiritually. The lifting up of our hands and arms also acknowledges our worship of the Creator as the Spirit that is much greater and wiser than ourselves. The raising of hands and arms in this manner always gives me a mental image of a small, needy child reaching for the comfort and safety of the grasp of a parent.

THE GOD ORGASM

The posture of lifting arms and hands can also be keeping your arms to your sides, and bending your lower arms and your hands to be parallel to the surface that you are standing on or sitting upon, with the palms open and facing up. This is supposedly the posture of prayer of the ancient Jews of the Bible, and I enjoy the mental picture of worship that the physical activity creates. Bent arms at the sides of your body, with hands extended out, and the palms pointed up to Heaven is again a symbol of expectation and the willingness to receive the message and Word of God. The open palms are once again asking God to bless us, and the mental side of the gesture is that we're inviting God to both lead and teach us as He chooses. In several ways, it seems more humbling and supplicative than simply reaching one's uplifted arms and hands to Heaven.

The danger of implementing any of the physical acts of worship that we have discussed is that they might seem insincere or trivial if we make any of them rote. But, I find that when you immerse yourself in the frame of mind of joyfully worshipping God, the physical acts of praising and glorifying Him become more natural and more spontaneous and sincere. In your prayer life, ask God to send His Spirit to you so that you can more naturally become a physical worshipper of God and the Lord Jesus Christ.

USE INSTRUMENTS TO JOYFULLY WORSHIP

A standing joke between my wife and I at the holiday seasons of Christmas and Easter is that I do not enjoy those services in my current home church as much as I did when I was a youth growing up in the Lutheran church. What is the reason for that? My wife always waits for me to begin to lament each such holiday that I miss brass instruments for the festive holiday worship, and the sounds they make to praise and glorify the Lord. My angst partly arises from the fact that I played the trumpet for many years of my public school education- I love the sound of the trumpet and its regal, festive tones. Trumpets invoke musical celebration and royal homage to my mind I suppose.

We have already noted in another, preceding chapter of this work that the Psalms encourage us to use musical instruments in the joyful praise and worship of God. "Rejoice in the LORD, O ye righteous: for praise is comely for the upright. Praise the LORD with harp: sing unto him with the psaltery and an instrument of ten strings. Sing unto him a new song; play skilfully with a loud noise." Psalm 33: 1-3. There is no better endorsement of actively praising and worshipping our God using music than to do it with a "loud noise." After all, since the time that all of us were toddlers, most of us probably enjoyed making any kind of noise and racket and tumult. I am striving to make my worship fun and joyful, and I hope you do too, so we should be able to make as much noise as we want in honoring and glorifying and worshipping our God.

Too much noise during our Sunday church services might well reach the point where it is a distraction to others, but I am all in favor of being led by the Spirit and being spontaneous with the noise that we are lifting up to our God. I've already told the story of the African heritage woman in my church who occasionally brings a tambourine to the church service. This wonderful and worshipful woman rattles her tambourine during the worship songs, and has a fun time with God while she does it. I keep waiting for her to play it during the pastor's sermon- it would be as robust and joyful as many choruses of "amens" or "hallelujahs."

I am somewhat of a self-taught piano player, just being able to pick out melodies and chords from my time as a trumpet player in my school band. As a result, I can sit down at the keyboard and find the tunes to old hymns, and even contemporary Christian songs sometimes. It's a fun way to worship God.

It may be more difficult for most of us to try to joyfully worship with a musical instrument. The guitar has become a common church worship band instrument in recent years. If you want to explore your musical side in worship, learn how to play one of these instruments. Buy a tambourine and shake it to the glory of God. Take up your own band instrument that you wish that you had learned to play as a child. Although I have never attempted to play one of the stringed instruments commonly found in orchestras, I have always been fascinated by the skill and dexterity exhibited by people proficient on the violin and cello and bass- the sounds that they create are gorgeous. The use of stringed instruments to worship and praise God has a beauty which is difficult to emulate in other forms of worship.

THE GOD ORGASM

Perhaps David again emphasized this point best in the Psalms, when he said, "Sing aloud unto God our strength: make a joyful noise unto the God of Jacob. Take a psalm, and bring hither the timbrel, the pleasant harp with the psaltery. Blow up the trumpet in the new moon, in the time appointed, on our solemn feast day. For this was a statute for Israel, and a law of the God of Jacob." Psalm 81: 1-4.

David was absolutely correct when he states in Psalm 81 that music is undoubtedly the most joyful part of worship to our God. Musical instruments are an integral part of making those melodies to our Father.

LIFT UP YOUR VOICE IN PRAISE AND WORSHIP

I sing in the worship choir at my church, which turns out to be a once a month time for our larger group of people to lead the Sunday morning worship and praise songs at the services at my church. For some reason, we are deemed not talented enough or capable enough to sing choir anthems alone. We collectively have a practice evening the Thursday before we sing, and I spend time throughout the week trying to memorize the music for each song. For a long time, I have regretted that we don't participate in choir once a week as in some churches, and we don't sing those choir-only anthems either.

While we are not collectively anywhere close to being professional singers, there are a solid group of very good voices in our choir, and it's a fun time for me. But, what I appreciate about participation in choir, even more than the actual performances, is the fact that the songs from my practices and then our Sunday morning choir worship time keep rolling through my head for the rest of the week. If the tune is particularly catchy and memorable on any given song, I find myself humming it as I go about my daily activities. If the song turns out to be a personal favorite, I walk around singing the tune, whether I'm alone in the house with my rambunctious Irish Setter, Ginger, or when my wife is also present. It's a great time of spontaneously praising and joyfully worshipping my God, just because my brain seems to love the musical nature of worship.

Psalm 96 vehemently agrees that lifting our voices to our God is an excellent way to worship Him. "O sing unto the Lorde a new song: sing unto the Lord, all the earth. Sing unto the Lord, bless his name, shew forth his salvation from day to day. Declare his glory among the heathen, his wonders among all people. For the Lord is great, and greatly to be praised: his is to be feared above all gods." Psalm 96: 1-4.

If you believe that you are not a candidate for your church choir, or any choir for that matter, sing to God regardless of your own opinion of your vocal talents. It is my firm belief that God loves, honors and respects our voices when they are lifted up to Him in joyful praise and worship, and that the quality of your voice doesn't really matter that much to Him. It's the effort, and the intent of the heart that count.

I always joke that I am an avid shower singer, for there is nobody in the cubicle with me to criticize or critique. It's just me enjoying making my own music, and using my bottle of liquid soap as a faux microphone.

If singing is still not your favorite thing to do, my other suggestion for you would be to immerse yourself in listening to praise and worship music over your radio or streaming device. I have developed the excellent habit of constantly having praise and worship music on and audible throughout the day, and I find that the same concept applies to just listening as well. After listening to praise and worship music,

I am still humming and singing the songs well after the radio or streaming device is turned off. It's yet another way to immerse myself in joyful worship to my God.

Lately I have also been personally blessed by just sitting down in my quiet place, turning on the streaming device to praise and worship music, and spending a quiet time of listening and reflecting on the words and meaning of each song. I might lift up my hands in worship, I might shut my eyes, but anytime that I do this it turns into a rather intense and enjoyable time spent with my God. And, yes, I find myself singing along to each song as it becomes familiar. As you can imagine, Ginger has become a big fan of praise and worship music, by necessity. She is without a doubt the most spiritual dog that I have ever owned- she was raised by and lived with an Amish family in northeast Ohio for the first four years of her life. Any time Ginger is left alone in the house when we go out, we always turn the streaming device to praise and worship music. Our dog needs the soothing, calming effect of spiritual tunes, if nothing else.

I would greatly recommend that you make vocal music and song a regular time of your worship time at home or office during the week, as yet another way to find joy in your time spent with God.

STUDY YOUR BIBLE

I love to read my Bible, and for years have had a regular habit and plan which I invoke for my study. My daily habit is to read a chapter from the first books of the Old Testament, then a Psalm, a chapter from one of the Gospels (I rotate them), and a chapter from Acts and the Epistles as I work through to the end of the New Testament. I also supplement this rotation by periodically reading the Old Testament prophets.

At first blush, just reading the Bible using such a plan doesn't necessarily seem to readily lend itself to joyful worship, particularly for veteran Christians such as myself who are very familiar with almost all parts of the Bible. But, I would urge you to use your imagination to make reading your Bible a time of joyful worship.

I would recommend taking the time during a Bible study session to study and reflect on each word and story, and to joyfully praise God for the miracles and influences He brought into the lives of the characters of the Bible who we meet along the way. I can find worshipful joy in viewing what God did in the lives of Abraham, Isaac, Jacob, Joseph and others. Conversely, there is also joy that can be discovered when God takes situations which seem to be bad, and works the circumstances out for the good of His children and for the glory and honor to Himself. In regard to making lemonade out of lemons, think of the trials of Joseph as he is thrown into prison, or the challenges of Job as his entire life is turned into chaos and havoc when he loses everything that he had due to the interference of Satan in his life. Job's response somehow echoed that idea of finding joy in even the most terrible of circumstances- "The Lord gave, and the Lord hath 1taketh away, blessed be the name of the Lord." Job 1: 21.

Very many verses from both sides of the Bible echo the joy that can be discovered in reading God's word. Perhaps one of the simplest, yet profound, statements from the Bible in this regard illustrates that reading the Book is joyful, because the words give us hope. "For whatsoever things were written aforetime were written for our learning, that we through patience and comfort of the scriptures might have hope." Romans 15: 4. Very often, my days need huge doses of hope as I learn of the needs and travails of friends and family, and peruse the day's news on my computer. Those items of need are in addition to whatever concerns occurring in my own life need to be addressed. I take great comfort that I can find that hope by turning to the pages of Scripture.

Similarly, King Solomon buttresses the thought that being constantly in the word of God provides goodness for all aspects of our lives. "My son, attend to my words; incline thine ear unto my sayings. Let them not depart from thine eyes; keep them in the midst of thine heart. For they are life unto those that find them, and health to all their flesh." Proverbs 4: 20-22.

In a similar vein, God also promises that the person who reads and studies His Word will prosper. "Blessed is the man that walketh not in the counsel of the ungodly, nor standeth in the way of sinners, nor sitteth in the seat of the scornful. But his delight is in the law of the LORD; and in his law doth he meditate day and night. And he shall be like a tree planted by the rivers of water, that bringeth forth his fruit in his season; his leaf also shall not wither; and whatsoever he doeth shall prosper." Psalm 1: 1-3.

If there is no other reason to study the Bible, King Solomon also makes it clear that the main joy of our lives should be to discover the knowledge of God. "Knowledge" is a great Word here, because it can mean both discovering the existence and power and might of God, as well as learning the teachings and wisdom of God through His Words in the Bible. "My son, if thou wilt receive my words, and hide my commandments with thee; So that thou incline thine ear unto wisdom, and apply thine heart to understanding; Yea, if thou criest after knowledge, and liftest up thy voice for understanding; If thou seekest her as silver, and searchest for her as for hid treasures; Then shalt thou understand the fear of the LORD, and find the knowledge of God." Proverbs 2: 1-5.

Jesus in His teachings also told us that studying His Words and the other Words of the Bible give us wisdom and stability. "Therefore whosoever heareth these sayings of mine, and doeth them, I will liken him unto a wise man, which built his house upon a rock." Matthew 7: 24.

By far, my favorite story of the impact of the Bible, and the joy that it should give us as we study and ruminate on God's

THE GOD ORGASM

word occurs in the book of Nehemiah. In that Book, we learn that, when a great deal of the population of Israel was carried off into captivity in Babylon, the Word of God was forgotten and removed from them. When the captives returned to Jerusalem, the story unfolds that the Priests once again taught the power and impact of the Word of God by bringing out the probably dusty Scrolls, and renewing and restoring the familiarity of the people to God's word.

"And all the people gathered themselves together as one man into the street that was before the water gate; and they spake unto Ezra the scribe to bring the book of the law of Moses, which the LORD had commanded to Israel. And Ezra the priest brought the law before the congregation both of men and women, and all that could hear with understanding, upon the first day of the seventh month. And he read therein before the street that was before the water gate from the morning until midday, before the men and the women, and those that could understand; and the ears of all the people were attentive unto the book of the law. And Ezra the scribe stood upon a pulpit of wood, which they had made for the purpose; and beside him stood Mattithiah, and Shema, and

Anaiah, and Urijah, and Hilkiah, and Maaseiah, on his right hand; and on his left hand, Pedaiah, and Mishael, and Malchiah, and Hashum, and Hashbadana, Zechariah, and Meshullam. And Ezra opened the book in the sight of all the people; (for he was above all the people;) and when he opened it, all the people stood up: And Ezra blessed the LORD, the great God. And all the people answered, Amen, Amen, with lifting up their hands: and they bowed their heads, and worshipped the LORD with their faces to the ground. Also Jeshua, and Bani, and Sherebiah, Jamin, Akkub, Shabbethai, Hodijah, Maaseiah, Kelita, Azariah, Jozabad, Hanan, Pelaiah, and the Levites, caused the people to understand the law: and the people stood in their place. So they read in the book in the law of God distinctly, and gave the sense, and caused them to understand the reading. And Nehemiah, which is the Tirshatha, and Ezra the priest the scribe, and the Levites that taught the people, said unto all the people, This day is holy unto the LORD your God; mourn not, nor weep. For all the people wept, when they heard the words of the law. Then he said unto them, Go your way, eat the fat, and drink the sweet, and send portions unto them for whom nothing is prepared:

THE GOD ORGASM

for this day is holy unto our LORD: neither be ye sorry; for the joy of the LORD is your strength. So the Levites stilled all the people, saying, Hold your peace, for the day is holy; neither be ye grieved. And all the people went their way to eat, and to drink, and to send portions, and to make great mirth, because they had understood the words that were declared unto them. And on the second day were gathered together the chief of the fathers of all the people, the priests, and the Levites, unto Ezra the scribe, even to understand the words of the law. And they found written in the law which the LORD had commanded by Moses, that the children of Israel should dwell in booths in the feast of the seventh month: And that they should publish and proclaim in all their cities, and in Jerusalem, saying, Go forth unto the mount, and fetch olive branches, and pine branches, and myrtle branches, and palm branches, and branches of thick trees, to make booths, as it is written. So the people went forth, and brought them, and made themselves booths, every one upon the roof of his house, and in their courts, and in the courts of the house of God, and in the street of the water gate, and in the street of the gate of Ephraim. And all the congregation of them that were come again out of the captivity made booths, and sat under the booths: for since the days of Jeshua the son of Nun unto that day had not the children of Israel done so. And there was very great gladness. Also day by day, from the first day unto the last day, he read in the book of the law of God. And they kept the feast seven days; and on the eighth day was a solemn assembly, according unto the manner." Nehemiah 8: 1-18.

Nehemiah 8 paints a vivid picture of the joy which the reading of God's Word should give us. The Jewish people, who had for so long been denied access to and knowledge of the Scriptures, were at first tearful at the hearing of the Word, undoubtedly in the stark realization of what they had lost and been denied over their years of captivity. But Nehemiah counseled the Israelites to be joyful in the Word of God, to celebrate its return, and, as a result, a great series of feast days and joyous celebrations occurred.

Remember the lessons and joys of Nehemiah 8 as you invoke the privilege of studying your Bible daily in joyful worship.

THE GOD ORGASM

PRAY AND PRAISE GOD DAILY

What can be more joyful and exhilarant in our worship than talking to our God? That is what prayer is in its most fundamental and elementary form- we have the privilege of having a dialogue with God so that we can praise Him, worship Him, tell Him our problems and triumphs, and ask Him to be working in our lives and the lives of others.

The Bible has much to say about prayer. First and foremost, the Word of God tells us to just do it. "Rejoice evermore. Pray without ceasing. In everything give thanks: for this is the will of God in Christ Jesus concerning you." I Thessalonians 5: 16-18. In a similar fashion, Colossians 4: 2 instructs us to, "Continue in prayer, and watch in the same with thanksgiving." Elsewhere, James, the earthly half-brother of Jesus, emphasized that prayer should be used for confession, and that it even has healing powers. "Confess your faults one to another, and pray for one another, that ye may be healed. The effectual, prayer of a righteous man availeth much." James 5: 16.

The best example that we should and need to pray daily is from Jesus Himself. All through the Gospels, Jesus uttered many prayers to His Father, and certainly prayed before doing anything of importance in His ministry. And, we have the promises of Jesus that our prayers will be answered by God, when we pray with righteous intentions and purposes. "Again I say unto you, That if two of you shall agree on earth as touching anything that they shall ask, it shall be done for them of my father which is in heaven. For where two or three are gathered together in my name, there I am in the midst of them." Matthew 18: 19-20.

For many of us, our biggest obstacle in prayer is not knowing or planning what to say when we go to our God. Jesus left us with instructions on how to pray as well, and what he left for us to study is a powerful outline of the mechanics of prayer. The words of the famous Lord's Prayer are as follows- "And it came to pass, that, as he was praying in a certain place, when he ceased, one of his disciples said unto him, Lord, teach us to pray, as John also taught his disciples. And he said unto them, When ye pray, say, Our Father which art in heaven, Hallowed be thy name. Thy kingdom come. Thy will be done, as in heaven, so in earth. Give us day by day our daily bread. And forgive us our sins; for we also forgive every one that is indebted to us. And lead us not into temptation; but deliver us from evil." Luke 11: 1-4

From my Lutheran background I have already spoken of in this work, we said the Lord's Prayer as a part of every church service. As a result, I believe that the Lord's Prayer can become rote, and something that is intoned without really thinking about the meaning and intentions of the words of the prayer. But, I love the Lord's Prayer as an outline of topics to use in your own joyful worship time and quiet time spent with God. If you don't know what to pray for as you pause to spend time with our Father, the Lord's Prayer demonstrates elements that we should always include in our prayer time. The topics of praise, worship, asking for daily needs, asking for the forgiveness of sins, and seeking protection from the wiles and influences of Satan are all found in the Lord's Prayer. Perhaps the most profound part of the prayer is that we should request the return of God's kingdom to our Earth- the second return of the Lord Jesus Christ.

Ray Eichenberger

I often fall into the trap of making the petition and requests portion of my prayer time exclusively a laundry list of things that I need, or that my immediate family needs. There is absolutely nothing wrong in doing so, but we also need to expand beyond what I very pejoratively call these "gimme" prayers (such as give me this, give me that). Instead, we should spend more time in our dialogues with God lifting up the needs of other people- friends, fellow church members, more distant relatives, our nation, our nation's leaders- the list is quite endless. One of the benefits of being active in my church, and a church small group, is that I always am made aware of the urgent needs of other people. At any given time, it is quite usual to be informed of the health concerns, family concerns, problems, and the travails of other people. The information about the prayer needs of others has often become so common and comprehensive that I have started to make lists on my cell phone memo app that I refer to while I am praying. And, praying for, and lifting up the needs of other people, becomes a joyful part of the worship time of prayer, as I feel very useful in asking God to work in the lives of my friends, relatives, and fellow church members.

THE GOD ORGASM

I must also say a word about verbal prayer, particularly in front of others. I was not at all used to verbal prayer in my church upbringing, and really didn't do much of it until, as an adult, I became a member of smaller Sunday School groups, and then later small groups in my church. If you're not used to doing so, verbal prayer in the presence of others might seem to be intimidating. I started out being very insecure and awkward feeling in verbal prayer in front of others, particularly when praying with people who are very talented in that area. Over the years I have prayed with quite a few people who usually sound like the best orators you have ever heard in your life. Invariably, there is someone praying in my circle who possesses a James Earl Jones type of cool, resonant voice and always seems to have relevant, pertinent, and eloquent things to say to our God.

But, shed your insecurities and awkwardness, and think of group, oral prayer time as simply a time of worship and joyful praise to God. In essence, this is like singing- you don't have to have the best voice in the world for God to appreciate and honor your acts of praise and worship when you lift up sincere prayers to Him. This is not an oratorical contest, but a time to enjoy communicating with and praising our God with others.

The importance of our prayers to our God, and the concurrent value and importance that God places on our prayers, is very chillingly and amazingly illustrated in the Book of Revelation. In Revelation, John was given the great privilege of being taken to Heaven, and observing scenes of worship and the worship activities in that Holy Place. The following gives a context to John's observation of the praise and worship occurring in Heaven, and ends with an insight as to the value and worth of our prayers in the eyes of our God. "And I saw in the right hand of him that sat on the throne a book written within and on the backside, sealed with seven seals. And I saw a strong angel proclaiming with a loud voice, Who is worthy to open the book, and to loose the seals thereof? And no man in heaven, nor in earth, neither under the earth, was able to open the book, neither to look thereon. And I wept much, because no man was found worthy to open and to read the book, neither to look thereon. And one of the elders saith unto me, Weep not: behold, the Lion of the tribe of Judah, the Root of David, hath prevailed to open the book, and to loose the seven seals thereof. And I beheld, and, lo, in the midst of the throne and of the four beasts, and in the midst of the elders, stood a Lamb as it had been slain, having seven horns and seven eyes, which are the seven Spirits of God sent forth into all the earth. And he came and took the book out of the right hand of him that sat upon the throne. And when he had taken the book, the four beasts and four and twenty elders fell down before the Lamb, having every one of them harps, and golden vials full of odours, which are the prayers of saints." Revelation 5: 1-8.

Think of the meaning of the last sentence of that portion of Revelation 5. Every prayer that we lift up to our God is kept, recorded, and stored in golden vials. Our prayers are described as pleasant odors, which are filed away and valued by God in Heaven. Every time I read that passage, I get goose-bumps, and am reminded of the immense value and importance of prayer.

EXPERIENCE THE BEAUTY OF NATURE AND PRAISE

I am a nature lover, and have had the privilege and opportunity to travel to many beautiful places in the United

States, the Caribbean, and other parts of the world. The meeting of the sea and land at the beach comes to mind in that regard. The mountains of Colorado, Wyoming, Montana, New Mexico, and Hawaii are also very beautiful. I have sat in awe at the Grand Canyon and just reveled in the beauty of what God created at that place. I recently visited a slot canyon near Lake Powell, Arizona, and marveled at the grandeur and diversity of the colors and vibrant shades that were created in that unusual place (the slot canyons are cave-like). The deserts of Nevada in their starkness also have a beautiful and quiet atmosphere. A recent trip to Yellowstone National Park and Grand Teton National Park not only revealed gorgeous scenery, but the opportunity to see many kinds of animals in the wild- gazing at the majestic bison was my favorite activity (no, we didn't go play with them or pet them to create a stupid tourist video).

I have had the privilege to visit Israel, which is a land of many diverse landscapes- stark desert, lush valleys, lakes, and streams. The Sea of Galilee is beautiful, as well as the Garden Tomb in Jerusalem, and the beauty was greatly enhanced by

THE GOD ORGASM

the awe and wonder of the thought that Jesus walked on the very parts of the land that I was visiting.

The beauty of nature created by God is also greatly enhanced by viewing the wild animals that reside on both the land and in the sea. I recently saw awesome humpback whales in Hawaii, as they breached the surface of the Pacific Ocean and majestically rose out of the water. Dolphins regularly appear at a place where I like to winter in Florida, and they are gorgeous and fascinating creatures to watch. I can remember sitting on a rock in the heights of the Rocky Mountains in Colorado, gazing for an hour or more at a herd of beautiful elk which were peacefully grazing in a placid, green meadow. The bison at Yellowstone National Park were magnificent, and I was amazed at the majesty and size of those creatures. I love horses, and have witnessed a herd of wild horses enjoying the freedom of open range lands in Nevada- they are gorgeous to watch, and even more beautiful when they run.

When I view such places and things, it immediately comes to my mind that we worship a Creator and God who has the power and ability to fashion and form the land, plants, and animals which provide such beautiful and pastoral scenes for us to view and enjoy. Paul in the Book of Romans reminds us that we know that God exists and is real when we view the beauty of His creation- "Because that which may be known of God is manifest in them; for God hath shewed it unto them. For the invisible things of him from the creation of the world are clearly seen, being understood by the things that are made, even his eternal power and Godhead; so that they are without excuse." Romans 1: 19-20. To paraphrase Paul, the order, beauty, and character of nature is sufficient in and of itself as proof for man that God exists.

The awe and wonder in worshipping God for the beauty of creation continues in many Bible verses. "The heavens declare the glory of God, and the firmament sheweth his handywork." Psalm 19: 1. This is a similar declaration to that of Paul in Romans 1: 19-20, and Paul may have been thinking of the Psalm when he penned his own lines.

"O Lord, ho manifold are thy works! In wisdom hast thou made them all: the earth is full of thy riches." Psalm 104: 24. "In his hand are the deep places of the earth: the strength of the hills is his also. The sea is his, and he made it: and his hands formed the dry land." Psalms 95: 4-5.

THE GOD ORGASM

"When I consider the heavens, the work of thy fingers, the moon and the stars which thou hast ordained: What is man that thou are mindful of him? And the son of man, that thou visitest him?" Psalms 8: 3-4. This and similar verses move my spirit when I consider that the grandeur and beauty of the creation of God often serves to just make me feel small and insignificant compared to the breadth of what God has created.

I have taken a number of cruises in my life, and that same feeling of awe-struck insignificance has enveloped me several times when I have stood at the railing of my ship and gazed upon the seemingly endless water of the ocean. Very often when at sea, there is nothing to view on the horizon except the vast expanses of open water. Once again, a Psalm echoes that very thought to us. "They that do down to the sea in ships, that do business in great waters; These see the works of the Lord, and his wonders in the deep." Psalm 107: 23-24. I once attended a wedding conducted at a very old sailor's chapel in New Bedford, Massachusetts, and that particular Bible verse was highlighted on the walls of the sanctuary. Men who spent their days sailing the ocean appreciated the beauty, awe, and the fearsome power of the seas upon which they sailed.

Other Bible verses clearly state that all of nature recognizes the beauty and creative ability of our God, and is subject to His control and power- animals, hills, and the ocean. "For every beast of the forest is mine, and the cattle upon a thousand hills. I know all the fowls of the mountains: and the wild beasts of the field are mine." Psalms 50: 10-11 "Fear ye not me? Saith the Lord: will ye not tremble at my presence, which have placed the sand for the bound of the sea by a perpetual decree, that it cannot pass it: and though the waves thereof toss themselves, yet can they not prevail, though they road, yet can not pass over it?" Jeremiah 5: 22 "For ye shall go out with joy, and be led forth with peace: the mountains and the hills shall break forth before you into singing, and all the trees of the field shall clap their hands." Isaiah 55: 12 "But ask now the beasts, and they shall teach thee; and the fowls of the air, and they shall tell thee: Or speak to the earth, and it shall teach thee: and the fishes of the sea shall declare unto thee. Who knoweth not in all these that the hand of the LORD hath wrought this? In whose hand is the soul of every living thing, and the breath of all mankind. Job 12: 7-10.

I am a huge fan of The Chosen series about the life of Jesus, and watching the now multiple seasons of that show reminds me that it was fitting that Jesus spent a great deal of time in His ministry out in nature- the Creator aptly enjoying His Creation. As a result, Jesus made the following rather famous observation about the grandeur of the animals and plants which He placed into our world. "Therefore I say unto you, Take no thought for your life, what ye shall eat, or what ye shall drink; nor yet for your body, what ye shall put on. Is not the life more than meat, and the body than raiment? Behold the fowls of the air: for they sow not, neither do they reap, nor gather into barns; yet your heavenly Father feedeth them. Are ye not much better than they? Which of you by taking thought can add one cubit unto his stature? And why take ye thought for raiment? Consider the lilies of the field, how they grow; they toil not, neither do they spin: And yet I say unto you, That even Solomon in all his glory was not arrayed like one of these." Matthew 6: 25-30.

One of my favorite things to do to enjoy God's creation and to experience the joy of worship in that medium is to take a chair and simply sit outside in nature and pray. It is also a great time to sing songs of worship to God, if you can get beyond the temporary insecurities of thinking that any other person who comes along may find your singing out in the woods a bit strange- if they were to say anything, it would be a great time to witness and share the Gospel. Take your chair to the seaside and pray and worship. Take your chair up to the mountains and sit and indulge in reveling in the natural beauty of the scenery and any animals who come by for you to view. Take your chair to the woods and spend time in prayer. One of my favorite poets is Robert Frost, and his work, Stopping By the Woods on a Snowy Evening, begins with the line, "Whose woods these are I think I know." Amen, Mr. Frost.

Conversely, I will never understand the mindsets of those people who believe in evolution, and who are convinced that the earth and its natural beauty and magnificent animals somehow came into existence from some slimy and teeming cauldron of goo. If the creative ability of God seems unlikely to some doubting types, why isn't it even more unlikely to believe that a swirling, toilet-like vat of chemicals spawned human beings, the beauty of nature and the gorgeous, wild beasts?

SHARE YOUR JOY WITH OTHERS

When we joyfully worship our God every day, that same joyful attitude should then carry over into everything that we do in our lives. As a result, our behaviors and attitudes should naturally attract other people to you and I, who should be able to recognize us as something different and people set apart.

If you exude this joyful attitude (I'm working on it, one of my personal reasons for writing this work), and do naturally draw people to yourself as a great friend and companion, the end result of such relationships should certainly be that you have many, many chances and opportunities to share the Gospel with your friends. And, the last great Commandment of Jesus to all of us on this Earth as He departed was to "go ye therefore, and teach all nations, baptizing them in the name of the Father, and of the Son, and of the Holy Ghost: Teaching them to observe all things whatsoever I have commanded you." Matthew 28: 19-20. The Great

Commission was not just a polite suggestion of the risen Lord Jesus Christ- it is a command.

The Apostle Peter took the Great Commission to heart in his life's work, since he devoted himself to being a traveling evangelist, and saw great fruit result from his labors. Peter also exhorted all of us to follow in his footsteps, "But sanctify the Lord God in your hearts: and be ready always to give an answer to every man that asketh you a reason of the hope that is in you with meekness and fear." I Peter 3: 15.

There is a promise in the Scriptures that the Holy Spirit will provide us words to say as we evangelize others. "But ye shall receive power, after that the Holy Ghost is come upon you: and ye shall be witnesses unto me both in Jerusalem, and in all Judaea, and in Samaria, and unto the uttermost part of the earth." Acts 1: 8. While we can certainly have peace in the promise that we are not alone as we talk to others about God and Jesus, it also helps to equip yourself with knowledge of God's word before you go out to evangelize. I am perhaps not the best Bible verse memorizer at my advancing age, but memorizing Scripture is a worthy task and goal.

THE GOD ORGASM

The other reason for preparing yourself to talk to others about God and Jesus is that evangelism is spiritual warfare. It requires prayer and knowledge of the Scriptures. Satan doesn't want other people to come to a saving knowledge about Jesus, and he will create roadblocks and obstacles in your way and in the way of your unsaved friends in order to prevent any fruits from your evangelistic efforts. How do we know that evangelism is spiritual warfare? Jesus very plainly told us that in the parable of the soils- "And when much people were gathered together, and were come to him out of every city, he spake by a parable: A sower went out to sow his seed: and as he sowed, some fell by the way side; and it was trodden down, and the fowls of the air devoured it. And some fell upon a rock; and as soon as it was sprung up, it withered away, because it lacked moisture. And some fell among thorns; and the thorns sprang up with it, and choked it. And other fell on good ground, and sprang up, and bare fruit an hundredfold. And when he had said these things, he cried, He that hath ears to hear, let him hear. And his disciples asked him, saying, What might this parable be? And he said, Unto you it is given to know the mysteries of the kingdom of

God: but to others in parables; that seeing they might not see, and hearing they might not understand. Now the parable is this: The seed is the word of God. Those by the way side are they that hear; then cometh the devil, and taketh away the word out of their hearts, lest they should believe and be saved." Luke 8: 4-12

SERVE OTHERS AND SHARE YOUR JOY IN GOD

One of the many excuses that I have heard about the failure to talk to other people about God and our faith in Jesus is lack of opportunity to meet other people. I have used this excuse in my own mind, when I consider that I would evangelize other people if I only had more frequent opportunities to meet more people. This issue seemed to be especially pronounced during the height of the Covid pandemic, when we were all told to isolate, work from home, and socially distance ourselves from others. During that time, I was even shocked that churches failed to have their regularly scheduled Sunday services. We did it later with advanced planning and some clever solutions to the problem- the services should not have stopped.

THE GOD ORGASM

In my own experiences, I have grown to realize that the best way to meet non-believers to tell them about Jesus is to go out into the world and serve others. The idea of serving other people is not just a fuzzy and kind suggestion from our Lord, but instead again comes by way of a commandment, and failure to do so may result in long term eternal repercussions.

"Then shall the King say unto them on his right hand, Come, ye blessed of my Father, inherit the kingdom prepared for you from the foundation of the world: For I was an hungred, and ye gave me meat: I was thirsty, and ye gave me drink: I was a stranger, and ye took me in: Naked, and ye clothed me: I was sick, and ye visited me: I was in prison, and ye came unto me. Then shall the righteous answer him, saying, Lord, when saw we thee an hungred, and fed thee? or thirsty, and gave thee drink? When saw we thee a stranger, and took thee in? or naked, and clothed thee? Or when saw we thee sick, or in prison, and came unto thee? And the King shall answer and say unto them, Verily I say unto you, Inasmuch as ye have done it unto one of the least of these my brethren, ye have done it unto me. Then shall he say also unto them on the left hand, Depart from me, ye cursed, into everlasting fire, prepared for the devil and his angels: For I was an hungred, and ye gave me no meat: I was thirsty, and ye gave me no drink: I was a stranger, and ye took me not in: naked, and ye clothed me not: sick, and in prison, and ye visited me not. Then shall they also answer him, saying, Lord, when saw we thee an hungred, or athirst, or a stranger, or naked, or sick, or in prison, and did not minister unto thee? Then shall he answer them, saying, Verily I say unto you, Inasmuch as ye did it not to one of the least of these, ye did it not to me." Matthew 25: 34-45.

Such service lends itself to actively talk to and interact with those who we are serving. And, the natural witnessing opportunities which results are the perfect times to inform those who we serve that we are doing the acts of kindness, service, and benevolence for them to demonstrate the joy that we have for our Lord and Savior, Jesus Christ.

Now that I am retired, I have found that a great way to fill some of my time (other than writing) is to serve people. I write this in the summer months, and in the past few weeks I have participated in several different activities of service. I

THE GOD ORGASM

enjoyed singing with my church choir at a nursing home down the street from my church in a concert for the residents. A week or so later, we went to an adjacent nursing home in the area and helped the residents plant flowers on their patio area. The flower event was great- the residents did not want to just watch as we planted the flowers. Instead, they dove right in, got their hands dirty, and worked with the flowers and the soil. Their eagerness to do most of the work then lent itself to a perfect opportunity to get to know each person, and to talk about Jesus with them. It was a great event.

I have also recently helped others in my church to prepare lunches for elementary school students during the summer months, which has now become a tradition after consecutive years of doing so. It may seem shocking, but there are children who don't get enough to eat when school is not in session, when they lose access to subsidized lunches at school. And, this is in a seemingly middle-class suburb of my city. For our week of service this past summer, we prepared over two hundred lunches a day for these children, which consisted of hot meals and not just a peanut butter sandwich and a bag of chips.

Jesus appropriately described these opportunities to serve others when He said, "Let your light so shine before men, that they may see your good works, and glorify your Father which is in heaven." Matthew 5: 16.

The Apostle Peter also taught that we give glory to God when we serve others. "And above all things have fervent charity among yourselves: for charity shall cover the multitude of sins. Use hospitality one to another without grudging. As every man hath received the gift, even so minister the same one to another, as good stewards of the manifold grace of God. If any man speak, let him speak as the oracles of God; if any man minister, let him do it as of the ability which God giveth: that God in all thing may be glorified through Jesus Christ, to whom be praise and dominion for ever and ever. Amen." I Peter 4: 8-11.

It should go without saying after a review of the above Bible verses that serving others should be undertaken with a joyful heart and spirit. If you are grudgingly performing service tasks, or if your heart and efforts really aren't into the spirit of the endeavor, it might well be evident and noticed by those that we are serving and doing good deeds on their behalf. Above all, as you serve others, never be afraid to communicate the fact to them that you are joyfully serving them because you have Jesus in your heart, and that God has commanded all of us to help and assist our fellow man.

HAVE SEX WITH YOUR PARTNER

I am going to include sex as a very important way to joyfully worship God. After all, the sex acts are all gifts from Him, and were given to us to experience pleasure in our lives.

The intentions of God towards marriage and sex are clearly set forth in Genesis 2, shortly after the world was created by His hand. And, the plan came about because God, in His great wisdom and knowledge, knew that the man he created would be lonely and not complete if he lacked a companion to share all of it with. "And the LORD God said, It is not good that the man should be alone; I will make him an help meet for him." Genesis 2: 18.

The blissful, euphoric, and idyllic scene of the man and the woman living in the Garden of Eden are then described in the concluding verses of Genesis 2. "And the LORD God caused a deep sleep to fall upon Adam, and he slept: and he took one of his ribs, and closed up the flesh instead thereof; And the rib, which the LORD God had taken from man, made he a woman, and brought her unto the man. And Adam said, This is now bone of my bones, and flesh of my flesh: she shall be called Woman, because she was taken out of Man. Therefore shall a man leave his father and his mother, and shall cleave unto his wife: and they shall be one flesh. And they were both naked, the man and his wife, and were not ashamed." Genesis 2: 21-25.

The concluding verses of Genesis 2 have always been some of my favorites because they can permit my mind's eye to run rampant with imagination. I can visualize Adam and Eve strolling around naked in the Garden of Eden, having constant and meaningful communication with God, and indulging in copious amounts of joyful sex together in their fantastic surroundings. If you consider living life with great gusto and enjoyment as a vital and important part of joyful worship to God, this seems like the epitome of that concept. Of course, leave it to man to mess up even the most idyllic of situations.

The idea of marital sex as a part of joyful worship of our God is also found in the writings of Paul, of all places.

Although this is not the place for a discussion of Paul and his ideas about living and marriage, the Apostle seemed to not give much importance to the institution of marriage. To be fair, Paul was much more involved in, and emphasized, saving souls and winning people to Jesus than enjoying the luxuries of life and the benefits of marriage. But, Paul had the following to say about the duty and obligation of married couples to enjoy sex together- and frequently, at that. "Now concerning the things whereof ye wrote unto me: It is good for a man not to touch a woman. Nevertheless, to avoid fornication, let every man have his own wife, and let every woman have her own husband. Let the husband render unto the wife due benevolence: and likewise also the wife unto the husband. The wife hath not power of her own body, but the husband: and likewise also the husband hath not power of his own body, but the wife. Defraud ye not one the other, except it be with consent for a time, that ye may give yourselves to fasting and prayer; and come together again, that Satan tempt you not for your incontinency." I Corinthians 7: 1-5.

I don't know if Paul would agree that the sexual aspect of marriage, and the act of having sex, are intricate parts of the joyful worship of God, but he instructed married couples that they should not deprive their partners of the pleasures of sex, so that they would not be tempted by Satan to look outside of marriage for that enjoyment. One of my favorite lines of the above passage is the part that instructs, if you are abstaining from sex with your partner, you should instead devote your time to prayer to God. I will use that to buttress my argument here- both sex and prayer are important and vital parts of the joyful worship of our God.

So, as a result of my hypothesis, grab your partner by the hand, lead him or her to the bedroom, and tell them that you are ready to worship God.

AN ETERNITY OF JOY

I mentioned the entry of the Ark into Jerusalem during the time of David, and the King dancing before the Ark, as one of my favorite examples of joyful worship in our Bible. Recall that my other favorite example of joyful worship was the tumultuous scene on the Mount of Olives on the original Palm Sunday when Jesus rode the donkey down the hillside to Jerusalem and the Temple, to the thunderous cries and adoration of the crowd who worshipped Him on that day.

But, it is also true that we have even more joyous forms of worship to look forward to as we go forward in our lives as Christians. Perhaps what will be the most joyful scene of worshipping our God in the future is explained by the Apostle John when he had his vision of what we will witness in Heaven after we have gone to be with the Lord. "After this I

Ray Eichenberger

looked, and, behold, a door was opened in heaven: and the first voice which I heard was as it were of a trumpet talking with me; which said, Come up hither, and I will shew thee things which must be hereafter. And immediately I was in the spirit: and, behold, a throne was set in heaven, and one sat on the throne. And he that sat was to look upon like a jasper and a sardine stone: and there was a rainbow round about the throne, in sight like unto an emerald. And round about the throne were four and twenty seats: and upon the seats I saw four and twenty elders sitting, clothed in white raiment; and they had on their heads crowns of gold. And out of the throne proceeded lightnings and thunderings and voices: and there were seven lamps of fire burning before the throne, which are the seven Spirits of God. And before the throne there was a sea of glass like unto crystal: and in the midst of the throne, and round about the throne, were four beasts full of eyes before and behind. And the first beast was like a lion, and the second beast like a calf, and the third beast had a face as a man, and the fourth beast was like a flying eagle. And the four beasts had each of them six wings about him; and they were full of eyes within: and they rest not day and night, saying,

THE GOD ORGASM

Holy, holy, holy, LORD God Almighty, which was, and is, and is to come. And when those beasts give glory and honour and thanks to him that sat on the throne, who liveth for ever and ever, The four and twenty elders fall down before him that sat on the throne, and worship him that liveth for ever and ever, and cast their crowns before the throne, saying, Thou art worthy, O Lord, to receive glory and honour and power: for thou hast created all things, and for thy pleasure they are and were created." Revelation 4: 1-11.

And, I am personally excited with my own theory that, when we get to Heaven, we will be able to intimately commune with God as He enters our bodies and becomes one with us in a spiritual sense.

I hope that you will be able to use this work to increase the joy in your day to day worship. Joyful worship is not just a task to perform on Sunday mornings at your church, but can and should be accomplished throughout your day to day living as you go about your appointed tasks.

In the final analysis, there is nothing more joyful about worship than making it a daily habit to spend quality time with God. Follow my advice, take a chair out to the woods, a scenic lake, or your backyard, and worship Him with prayer, Bible study, and song. Be bold and take along a loud instrument to both enhance the joy of your worship and play it to God. When your neighbors ask you what in the world you are doing, you have created the perfect opportunity to witness to them and spread the Gospel.

Most of all, we have the hope and assurance from our God that the most joyful part of our worship of Him still awaits us in the future when we all arrive in Heaven and will be privileged to spend an eternity with God and the Lord Jesus Christ.

ABOUT THE AUTHOR

Ray Eichenberger is a retired attorney and lives in a suburb of Columbus, Ohio. Ray has a B.S. in Education from Miami University, a B.A. in History from Miami University, and a Juris Doctor from Capital University in Columbus, Ohio.

Ray's hobbies are golf, traveling, and racing his growing stable of harness horses. The highlight of his travels has been a recent trip to Israel. Ray has three children, and four grandchildren. Ray's four-legged daughter is a re-homed, rambunctious Irish Setter named Ginger.

The writing bug has hit Ray, and his other works include the following non-fiction books: <u>Harry Potter and the Gospel of Christ</u>; <u>God, the Law, and American Injustice</u>; <u>The P.E.A.C.E. of Christmas</u>; <u>The P.O.W.E.R. of Easter</u>, <u>Love,</u>

Ray Eichenberger

<u>Lust and Passion- Sex in the Bible</u>, <u>God is Alive, Why Am I So Dead?</u>, <u>Tears, Tragedy and Triumph</u>, <u>Death in the Bible</u>, <u>Thirsting for Jesus</u>, and <u>Sinners, Slaves or Saints- Women in the Bible</u>. Ray has now written seven other fictional works as well, a first novel, <u>The Blood of the Shroud</u>, and a sequel to that work, <u>The Seed of the Shroud</u>. Both of those books in the series deal with the Shroud of Turin. The third book of fiction is a continuation of the Shroud series, but a fun salute to thoroughbred horse racing which still has several spiritual messages- <u>Red Foot Jesse</u>. The fourth book of the Shroud Series, <u>The Heir of the Shroud</u>, follows a Christian President of the United States as she battles the United States Supreme Court over the topic of gay marriage. Another novel, <u>Sophia's Attic</u>, tells the story of a Jewish teenager sheltered by a Catholic married couple in Paris during World War II, and is based on a compilation of true stories. Following the recent trip to Israel, Ray also wrote a novel of intrigue in Jerusalem, <u>The Blood of Temple Mount.</u> The most recent novel, <u>The God Gene,</u> relates the tale of a young adult daughter whose life is thrown into turmoil after her deceased father sends her a genetic testing <u>kit as his final Christmas present to her.</u>

THE GOD ORGASM

Other new book titles published by Ray include a trilogy of novels based upon the Christmas story. A 2022 book featured the tale of the Magi who visited Jesus bearing their treasures- The Gifts Redeemed. The 2023 Christmas book, The Lamb Redeemed, tells the Christmas story from the viewpoint of a shepherd who was visited by the angels on the night that Jesus was born and found him in Bethlehem; the work also has the shepherd boy following the ministry of Jesus as an adult. A 2024 Christmas book, The Girl Redeemed, will add to the holiday series of novels based on the birth of Jesus, and features the story of Mary, the mother of Jesus.

A new non-fiction work, Why I'm A Christian. is written for seekers of God and new Christian,s and explains the author's reasons for his faith and the hope in God and Jesus that all of us have.

Also published in 2024 is a new novel set in Jerusalem titled The Blood of the Ark, a plot about a frantic search to find the Ark of the Covenant so that the new Temple in Jerusalem can open for worship. The Blood of the Ark is a plot sequel to the award winning The Blood of Temple Mount (The Santa Barbara International Film Festival). Already under way is a sequel to <u>The Blood of the Ark</u>, to be tentatively titled <u>The Blood of the Bones</u>, about a plot to undermine the very foundations of Christian beliefs.

Ray can be contacted at RedFootBooks@aol.com.

Follow Ray on Facebook at Red Foot Books.